Philosophy Meets the Infant

Infancy research and philosophy explore "first things," yet few books bring the two fields into contact. Stephen Langfur's *Philosophy Meets the Infant* integrates groundbreaking infancy studies of the last 50 years to offer a fresh exploration of our drive for human connection. He begins with a new understanding of self-awareness, which he locates in reciprocal attention between baby and caregiver. Instead of "I think, therefore I am," the new research supports "You attend, therefore I am." The event of becoming self-aware through another is termed a "You-I Event."

The idea is counterintuitive: we are perfectly self-aware when alone! To explain the change after infancy, Langfur makes transformative use of an old psychoanalytic finding. With the onset of language, a child internalizes (introjects) the most important You's, playing them toward herself in speech. Instead of the original You-I Event, we have its counterfeit in our heads. Nevertheless, a longing for the true Event persists in the unconscious; individual chapters trace this longing in work, love, art, conversation, and religion.

Organized into three parts ("The You-I Event in infancy and why it disappears," "The You-I Event after infancy," and "Philosophical Issues"), this book will be of keen interest to philosophers, infancy researchers, and anyone seeking new light on the major questions of human existence.

Stephen Langfur, PhD, has published widely in phenomenology and psychology journals. *Philosophy Meets the Infant* is Langfur's first book-length treatment of what he calls the You-I Event, in which self-awareness originates and develops through the attentions of others. He has also authored the philosophical memoir *Confession from a Jericho Jail* (Grove-Weidenfeld 1992, Fomite 2023).

Philosophy & Psychoanalysis Book Series
Jon Mills
Series Editor

Philosophy & Psychoanalysis is dedicated to current developments and cutting-edge research in the philosophical sciences, phenomenology, hermeneutics, existentialism, logic, semiotics, cultural studies, social criticism, and the humanities that engage and enrich psychoanalytic thought through philosophical rigor. With the philosophical turn in psychoanalysis comes a new era of theoretical research that revisits past paradigms while invigorating new approaches to theoretical, historical, contemporary, and applied psychoanalysis. No subject or discipline is immune from psychoanalytic reflection within a philosophical context including psychology, sociology, anthropology, politics, the arts, religion, science, culture, physics, and the nature of morality. Philosophical approaches to psychoanalysis may stimulate new areas of knowledge that have conceptual and applied value beyond the consulting room reflective of greater society at large. In the spirit of pluralism, *Philosophy & Psychoanalysis* is open to any theoretical school in philosophy and psychoanalysis that offers novel, scholarly, and important insights in the way we come to understand our world.

Titles in this series:

William James and Sigmund Freud on the Mind: Saving Subjectivity
Alfred I. Tauber

Jung & Spinoza: Passage Through The Blessed Self
Robert Langan

Philosophy Meets the Infant: How New Research Transforms the Understanding of Human Existence
Stephen Langfur

Philosophy Meets the Infant

How New Research Transforms the
Understanding of Human Existence

Stephen Langfur

Routledge
Taylor & Francis Group

LONDON AND NEW YORK

Cover image: Jill Sauve on Unsplash

First published 2025
by Routledge
4 Park Square, Milton Park, Abingdon, Oxon OX14 4RN

and by Routledge
605 Third Avenue, New York, NY 10158

Routledge is an imprint of the Taylor & Francis Group, an informa business

© 2025 Stephen Langfur

British Library Cataloguing-in-Publication Data
A catalogue record for this book is available from the British Library

ISBN: 9781032895291 (hbk)
ISBN: 9781032895277 (pbk)
ISBN: 9781003543275 (ebk)

DOI: 10.4324/9781003543275

Typeset in Times New Roman
by codeMantra

For Roni Ben Efrat

One day, the things I had gone through with her and learned about her came together and crystallized, and I saw her. All my life I'd been with human beings, obviously, but it was a revelation. It was the simple fact that she is this person, different from me, occupying her spaces, pursuing her pursuits. Suddenly it seemed marvelous and strange that she had chosen to be with me.

Contents

Part 1

The You-I Event in infancy and why it disappears

Introducing the You-I Event

The question that goaded me into philosophy has been asked in many ways—for instance, by Peggy Lee in a song entitled: "Is that all there is?" The question implies an expectation of more.

What is missing, I will argue, is a kind of connection to other people that we had as infants. I will reconstruct it and show how we lost it. Unconsciously, a yearning for it persists, finding indirect expression in work, love, dreams, art, conversation, ethics, and religion.

The lost connection may be described quite simply: by attending to me, other people make me aware of my existence and keep me so. No you, no I.

The idea appears to be contradicted by experience: each of us is self-aware when alone! But experience after infancy is not the last word. Its authority is shaken by a paradox.

The paradox of self-awareness

Think of a camera snapping a photo of a tree. Now suppose that in the very moment of snapping, the camera's mechanism makes a photo of itself snapping the photo, tree included. Is such a camera conceivable? Probably not, but consider the self. When I perceive a tree, I am also aware of myself perceiving it. This self-awareness is often dim. I can intensify it by switching the focus of attention from the tree to myself. In doing so, I am reflecting on myself. Ordinarily, however, self-awareness requires no special act of reflection. In being aware of anything, I am aware of myself being aware of it.

When we try to understand self-awareness, we come up against a paradox: How can the self, as *object* of awareness, be the *subject* that is aware of it? Immanuel Kant deemed this puzzle "impossible to explain, although it is

DOI: 10.4324/9781003543275-2

an undoubted fact …." (Kant 2002, 362). Sigmund Freud put the problem as follows:

> We wish to make the ego the matter of our enquiry, our very own ego. But is that possible? After all, the ego is in its very essence a subject; how can it be made into an object? Well, there is no doubt that it can be. The ego can take itself as an object, can treat itself like other objects, can observe itself, criticize itself, and do Heaven knows what with itself. In this, one part of the ego is setting itself over against the rest.
>
> (Freud 1964, 58)

Freud sidesteps the puzzle. "The ego can take itself as an object," but does "itself as an object" include its *being aware*? No, *being aware* belongs exclusively to the subject. If I try taking distance on myself to get a view of myself as aware, presto! a new *I* has arisen—the one who took distance. To view this new *I*, I must take distance again, and so on forever. It seems that I can never quite be aware of myself as aware. And yet I am, even in the simple act of perceiving a tree.

Our models of awareness are based on our experiences. The model of subject and object collapses under the fact of self-awareness. That may lead us to suspect that there is something wrong with the model—or worse, with the experiences.

Martin Heidegger, a century ago, showed the deficiency of the subject-object model *and* of the experiences on which it is based. After quoting the passage from Kant on the "undoubted fact," he proposed that "the Dasein" (his term for a human being, which I will explain in Chapter 5) "never finds itself otherwise than in the things themselves, and in fact in those things that daily surround it …." (Never otherwise. Not, for example, by viewing itself as an object.) "[R]ather, as the Dasein gives itself over immediately and passionately to the world itself, its own self is reflected to it from things" (Heidegger 1988, 159).

The first "thing" to which a human being "gives itself over immediately and passionately" is another human being. This fact will be our clue for solving the paradox of self-awareness.

Solution: The You-I Event

From the age of 4 months, babies distinguish between things they can reach and things they cannot. To do so, they must have "a sense of self not only as differentiated … but also as situated in relation to what the environment affords for action ….” (Rochat 2009, 96). What has made them self-aware so early?

Let us suppose that an even younger baby has yet to become self-aware. Imagine her experience during reciprocal attention with a caregiver (henceforth *carer*). Any form of such attention will do, but for now let it be the most common and powerful: mutual gaze, which begins soon after birth (Farroni et al. 2002). The carer is gazing into the baby’s eyes and the baby is gazing back. What does the baby see?

You might think that the baby sees nothing but a bunch of sense impressions. If that were the case, how would she ever come to know that they are part of a person with a mind? (This is the so-called *other-minds problem*.) At 2–5 days after birth, however, when a schematic face first seems to look straight at a baby and then to shift its eyes, the baby’s eyes follow (Farroni et al. 2004).[1] It is as if the baby has a reaction like the one we have when we see someone peering into the sky: we assume the person is looking at something and feel a pull to look too. The tendency appears in the animals of many species: on seeing a head and eyes turn in this or that direction, theirs follow. In the cases of ravens, rooks, dogs, wolves, four species of monkey, and the great apes, if you gaze toward a thing that is hidden from them by a barrier, they will move around it to see what you are looking at (Zeiträg et al. 2022, 17; on the great apes, Moll and Tomasello 2007). They know you are looking, and looking means looking *at something*.

The trait makes evolutionary sense: among prey and predator species, there is a survival advantage in seeing not just yellow discs but gazing eyes (there! among the reeds!). Apparently, natural selection solved the other-minds problem well before philosophers thought of it (Sloman and Chrisley 2003). I will say more about evolution in Chapter 2.

Armed with that much, we return to our question. Suppose that a baby has yet to become self-aware. The carer is gazing into the baby’s eyes and the baby is gazing back. What does the baby see?

The baby sees the carer *looking at something*. The baby cannot see this *something* but feels it. It is the manifestation of self.

---

1 For this to work, the baby must see the motion of the pupils. Before trying it on your baby, read Hood et al. (1998). On pupil motion as a factor, see Astor et al. (2021).

That is the core of the argument, so let me dwell here a moment. At any age, I know what I am feeling without needing to perceive my face or gestures. This is a distinctive feature of my own self as compared to others (I *do* need to perceive their behavior to sense what they feel). A sheer feeling, however, does not suffice to make me aware of myself: if we examine a feeling just as it occurs, nothing in it suggests the existence of an entity that is feeling it. During reciprocal attention, however, the carer's gaze does suggest the existence of an entity, a *something* she is looking at, and precisely where her gaze is focused a feeling is felt (perhaps several feelings at once: joy at being looked at, hunger, an itch). Voilà! the self.

Granted, there is more to self-awareness than that. We will see in Chapter 3 that the awareness of oneself as embodied, active, and continuous also comes about through interactions with a carer. The implication is radical: unlike a Cartesian subject ("I think, therefore I am"), I depend on others for awareness of my existence. You attend, therefore I am.

This dispels the paradox. In self-awareness, the object is not myself. If we insist on the terminology of subject and object, *you* are the object (nothing paradoxical about that!). Ordinarily, however, in speaking of an object, we mean an item that appears to a pre-existing subject—which is not the case here. You are present as attending, I am co-present as the target of that attending. I am one end of a loop. The event of becoming self-aware through another's attending will be termed a *You-I Event*.[2]

Someone objects: "Your answer may dispel the paradox for infants, but the rest of us undergo no such event and are perfectly self-aware." Later in this chapter, and more fully in Chapter 4, I will argue that the You-I Event is the main source of self-awareness after infancy too—with a twist.

There are numerous questions and objections, which will be taken up as we proceed. Here is one: "Many nonhuman animals are self-aware. Do they experience You-I Events?" I see no reason to deny the Event to animals engaging in reciprocal attention. Yet many may have an alternative source, whether in addition or instead. We will see in Chapter 10 that self-locomotion can produce self-awareness. This cannot be the principal solution for humans, though. As said, we are self-aware by the age of 4 months, before we can crawl.

***

2 I have developed the You-I account in five articles: Langfur (2013, 2014, 2016, 2019, 2023).

I asked us to imagine, for starters, a very young baby who is not self-aware. But can more be said about her age at the time of the first You-I Event?

One study suggests that reciprocal attention already occurs between the mother-to-be and the fetus, with touch as the principal medium (Marx and Nagy 2015; see also the Appendix, Challenge 1). I have chosen to start with postnatal self-awareness because the research is abundant. In either case, the recurring You-I loop is decisive. For the self is not a substance; it cannot exist on its own, but must constantly be recreated, whether in the womb, in infancy, or later.

Second, mutual gaze while breastfeeding has been found at 3 days, although by the age of 1 month it lasts longer (Lavelli and Poli 1998). Eva Simms writes:

> Newborn eyes can see the perfect distance of twelve inches: the bull's eye of the breast's aureole and the maternal face. Infants love to gaze at their mothers, a gaze that is one with the rhythm of breathing, sucking, and swallowing ....
>
> (Simms 2008, 14)

If some have doubts about those earlier ages, we can be confident that the You-I Event occurs by the infant's 8th week. At this age, when the carer mirrors the baby's expressions, the baby coos and smiles (Murray et al. 2016). Here is an excerpt from the maternal diary of infancy researcher Vasudevi Reddy:

> Shamini: 7 weeks, 5 days: It feels ... I can *make* her smile whenever I want—almost whatever mood she's in (not a frenzy or a raging hunger though!). Today for example—she's (in the beginning stages of) crying—she's looking off to the side—while I'm changing her. I take my attention away from the nappy and talk to her and smile (i.e., I make one burst of ... effort to catch her attention); she turns to me—mouth pulled down, crying stops for a few seconds, she smiles quiveringly, then grumbles/complains (rather than cries) with mouth down, still looking into my eyes.
>
> (Reddy 2008, 101)

By this age, surely, if not before, Shamini perceives her mother as more than a packet of sense impressions. She sees her as looking, smiling, and vocalizing—with herself as the target.

***

Here is another objection: "The You-I account entails an absurdity: when you-the-carer turn your attention elsewhere, I-the-baby must cease to exist for myself!" We will see in Chapter 3 that by my 3rd month, the items that are present during our exchanges continue to be *associated* with you after you have turned away or left the room. Supported by the associations, the memory of you attending and the hope of your return preserve a form of self-awareness. Lacking, to be sure, is the *something* which your attending made present. It too persists as a memory and a hope. The emptiness created by memory and hope can be filled, in part, by *effects* I make on things, which in some ways resemble your responses.

That softens the absurdity, but I do not want to soften it much. With all due respect to associations, memory, and hope, if you-the-carer are absent longer than a certain time, a switch occurs. The associated things then keep you present as *not* attending to me, and I become aware of myself as *not attended to*. It is the negative You-I Event. I sense the possibility of not being.

Nicholas of Cusa said to God: "And if You were to withdraw Your countenance from me, I would not at all continue to exist" (Hopkins 1985, 685). Ultimately, the same is true for a baby in relation to a carer.

With the words *not being* and *existence*, we enter a region where philosophy and infancy meet. The meeting has been long in coming, for the simple reason that philosophers, like everyone else, do not remember what life was like before they could speak. Since the 1970s, however, new ways of posing questions to babies, aided by new technologies, have made the first two years more accessible (Stern 1985, 38–42).

The counterfeit You-I Event

This book hinges on two ideas. The first is the account just given, which I will defend in Chapters 2 and 3: the main path to the I must loop through a You. But that is quite far from the kind of self-awareness adults know. Here the second idea comes in: You-I Events are the source of self-awareness after infancy too, but *in a counterfeit mode*. I analyze this mode briefly now and more fully in Chapter 4.

***

Evolutionary factors have resulted in babies who take joy in You-I Events (see Chapter 2). However, the intervals between Events are tinged with *dread of separation* (Bowlby 1960). Once I-the-child can speak, I am able to quell this dread. For I can talk to myself like you-the-carer while hearing as me.

For example, after her father has put her to bed and left the room, 2-year-old Emily repeats, in his intonation, things he said to her minutes before, including "Big kids like Emmy don't cry" (Dore 1989, 231ff). By the close imitation that language makes possible, I-the-child can play your part toward myself as an actor plays a character. Thus I feel attended to as if by you. The result is a sense of self. It is a thin version of the original, since the speaker is not really you, as I well know. The bestowal of this thinner self is entirely in my power, and so the suspense of the You-I Event is missing. Furthermore, in playing you toward myself I *pretend* that there is space between "us." The pretend space is the first mental interior.

Self-talk comes in many forms and functions, but in this book, except when a broader sense is specified, the term means playing the part of another person talking or listening to me. When the talk becomes inaudible to others (often in the early school years), we may call it *inner speech* (Duncan and Tarulli 2009). The played other will not save me from alligators, but it saves me from depending on real others for awareness that I exist. That is why inner speech "is reassuringly or irritatingly *there on tap* …. It offers us the unfailing if ambiguous company of a guest who does not plan to leave" (Riley 2004, 58).

***

Since self-talk is entirely up to me, we may term its result *the secure self.* I-the-child, -adolescent, and -adult play certain people toward myself so often that "they" become habitual inner companions. Philosopher Allan Køster writes: "[W]e develop a habituated felt sense of concrete others as part of embodied selfhood" (2021, 57). They are, in the words of Charles Fernyhough, "the people we carry with us" (2016, 32). I will term them *mock others*—mock as in simulated.

Mock others and the secure self together form a composite: the *subject*. ("Cogito ergo sum" is self-talk, reassuring me of my existence.) Flesh-and-blood others, no longer needed for self-awareness, are among the subject's *objects*. The subject is like a solar system, with the secure self in the center, surrounded by mock others who attend to it, all moving together as a unit through a universe of objects.[3]

---

3 If this derivation of the subject is correct, we should avoid the term *intersubjectivity* for the period prior to self-talk.

Mock others do not just speak or listen to me. They also attend with me in silence to things outside our loop. Their attention is modeled on the *joint attention* that occurs when people attend simultaneously to a third thing *and* each other, as attested by quick reciprocal smiles or glances. For example, when a carer and a 12-month-old play with a toy, attention is no longer like a spotlight on a single entity, but more like a bath of light encompassing three. I-the-baby see the thing, I am aware of you seeing it, and I am aware of you aware of me seeing it. When you turn your eyes from me toward it, I still feel attended to by you.

In a similar way, a mock other can attend with me to a third thing without lessening attention to me. When I enjoy the breeze, my mock others enjoy it with me. When I run from the avalanche, I appeal to them ("Mother!"). When I perceive a tree, they are quietly or noisily with me, attending to it and me. In its relation to objects, the subject has a joint-attentional structure.

This inner structure enables a new answer—a post-infancy answer—to the paradox with which we began: How can the self, as *object* of awareness, be the *subject* that is aware of it? Just as a carer and baby remain attentive to each other while jointly attending to a toy, mock others and I remain attentive to each other while jointly attending to things outside our inner loop. The result is the dim, proto-reflective, secure self-awareness of everyday life after infancy. To sharpen it by an act of reflection, I re-enliven my playing of the other (breaking through the automaticity of habit), and I observe myself from that mock point of view while continuing to look at the tree. This act of reflection is experienced as stepping back and examining oneself, but the position one steps back to is familiar: it is the position of a mock other. The act is performed in pretend space, which has become an integral part of the space in which one lives.

***

After I-the-child have mastered self-talk, suppose you re-enter the room. You do not appear in your former power as bestower of self-awareness. No one does or can. I have usurped your power by playing you toward myself. Because of the greater security it affords, self-talk is always out ahead, *precluding* the potential You in each encounter. The original kind of human connection goes into eclipse.

Self-talk restructures experience. The gains are immense: by the age of 3 years, separation anxiety eases; playing you-the-carer toward myself, I can regulate myself as you would; I can take multiple perspectives; I can begin the process of joining the larger social group, adopting its norms and values; I can carry the culture in my head (Tomasello 2019, 153). These developments are rightly extolled—they are part of becoming human—but we must note a negative aspect: in self-talk, one loses the fully important other and the self that is her gift. Life is safer, life is duller. There remains a yearning for what has been lost, but it is stymied by dread of reverting to absolute dependence.

The yearning and dread are excluded from awareness because of the change in structure: as a subject relating to objects, I cannot switch back to an altogether different way of being. We may speak, therefore, of a *split-off self* that yearns for the You-I Event while dreading it. Hence an occasional restlessness, which leads us to seek out avatars of the You. Hence too the homesickness that motivates a certain kind of philosophy. In answer to Peggy Lee's question, the world after self-talk is not all there is.

The rest of the book

This chapter has outlined the basic argument of the You-I account. In the remaining chapters of Part 1, I will present empirical evidence to support it.

In Part 2, Chapters 5–9, I trace the unconscious yearning for the You-I Event. The fields of love, dream, work, art, and conversation are *openings* through which that yearning infiltrates the structure created by self-talk.

In Chapter 10 of Part 3, I evaluate other attempts to explain self-awareness, including those by J. J. Gibson, Edmund Husserl, and Dan Zahavi. In Chapter 11, I apply the You-I account to the question of free will; in Chapter 12, to morality; in Chapter 13, to faith in a benevolent, omniscient, omnipotent God.

The You-I Event is not rare for a baby. To explain why it becomes so, I point to self-talk. But when its rarity is explained in this way, it seems impossible to attain. For who can expel the mock others that roost in our rafters, chattering away or silently looking on? Chapter 14 discusses what can be done.

In an Appendix, I consider objections to the You-I account from various fields, including autism research, theory of mind, multicultural studies, and research on inner speech.

***

Cogitor ergo sum. I am thought of, therefore I am.

2

Born to connect

The basic idea of the You-I account is not new. A century ago, Martin Buber wrote: "A human being becomes I through a You."[1] The idea permeates Colwyn Trevarthen's research on infants; he writes, for example: "It is in the nature of human consciousness to experience being experienced" (1993, 121). Vasudevi Reddy speaks of "a self first known as an object through experiencing oneself as an attentional and emotional object to another" (2008, 125).

There are some, nonetheless, who hold that one cannot be aware of other minds without first being self-aware: I have direct access to no mind other than my own; when I see a body that looks and behaves like mine, I impute to it a mind like mine.

This *analogy theory* does not persuade—at least not if we agree that babies are aware of other minds (namely, of carers attending to them). For a baby's body, as perceived by herself, is vastly dissimilar to the bodies around her.[2]

One way to resolve the difference is to hold that the analogy is unconscious. Cognitive scientist Alvin Goldman distinguishes between low-level and high-level mindreading (in this context, *mindreading* means attributing mental states to other entities). The low-level sort is "comparatively simple, primitive, automatic, and largely below the level of consciousness" (Goldman 2006, 113). In it, "perception of the target's face 'directly' triggers (subthreshold) activation of the same neural substrate of the emotion

---

1 *Der Mensch wird am Du zum Ich* (Buber 1995/1923, 28). Unless otherwise noted, all translations from German are mine.
2 Reciprocal vocalizations are not dissimilar. Might they be a basis for analogy? I discuss the issue in Chapter 10.

DOI: 10.4324/9781003543275-3

in question." He calls this *unmediated resonance*, suggesting that mirror neurons have a part in it.[3] Now, if such resonance occurs below the threshold of consciousness, there is room for the You-I Event above it. Evolution, we will see, has primed the newborn baby to recognize a carer attending. The baby need not synthesize sense impressions and then infer a mind behind them.

Speaking of a frightened man, Ludwig Wittgenstein wrote, "In general, I do not surmise fear in him—I *see* it. ...[I]t is as if the human face were in a way translucent ...." (1980, §170). True, the other may be feigning fear, but if so, he is exploiting the directness with which we are accustomed to perceive fear in others.

The founder of phenomenology, Edmund Husserl, also acknowledged that we perceive other people directly as experiencers (1989, 246–56, 384–85). His followers took up the point, beginning with Edith Stein. She writes that our awareness of other experiencers is *sui generis*, that is, not derived from other forms of awareness (Stein 1989, 11).

The ability to experience being experienced has a background in evolution, to which we now turn.

Human evolution

The social insects are famous for cooperative breeding, aka alloparenting, in which relatives help the mother to care for her infant from birth until maturity. Among bird species, about 9% practice it, among mammal species about 3%. Among *primates*, however, only two groups breed cooperatively: ours and a family of small-brained New World monkeys called Callitrichidae (Hrdy and Burkart 2020). According to Sarah Hrdy (2009), alloparenting has been our practice at least since *Homo erectus* emerged about two million years ago in Africa. For other great-ape mothers, the idea of letting anyone take part in caring for the baby in the first half year is anathema; even beyond that limit, mother and child are in continual contact until the latter can forage on its own at age 5 or 6. Why did our hominin forebears depart from this rule?

---

3 Goldman (2006, 127; on mirror neurons, 133ff.). Mirror neurons discharge both when one performs a motor act and when one observes a similar act performed by another. As to whether they are present in human newborns, the jury is still out.

The answer has to do with heavy accumulations of ice at the Earth's poles lasting thousands of years. The ice absorbed much of the water in the atmosphere, causing drought in the African tropics where hominins evolved. The jungles shrank. Among the species that survived, each had its own methods. A principal hominin method was the cooperative breeding mentioned above. The result went far beyond mere survival, however. The provisioning hands of fathers, grandmothers, older siblings, aunts, and others allowed many years for brain growth before the recipient was required to pull her weight as an adult in a large and complex group. Unlike the brains of other mammals, that of a human newborn has most of its growth ahead: at birth it is a fifth of adult size (Tomasello 2019, 25–26). Consequently, carers have exceptional influence on the tuning and pruning of neurons. By the age of 8, the brain has reached 90% of adult size, but the prefrontal cortex—essential in a large and complex group—is not fully formed until age 24 (Arain et al. 2013). In turn, the members of a large and complex group had better chances to discover techniques that provided food for brain growth (e.g., language, trapping, control of fire, cooking). Brain size and group size evolved in tandem. The most viable human group consists of 150 direct acquaintances, almost triple the size of a typical chimpanzee group. Human brain size is also triple that of chimpanzees (Dunbar 2014, 66–74).

Because the availability of alloparents enabled mothers to wean their children at 3 years rather than the usual great-ape 5, hominins reproduced more often. Separations from the mother, writes Hrdy, confronted the infant with "chronic challenges and uncertainties," which

> caused little [human] apes, already endowed [like nonhuman apes] … with the neural equipment for rudimentary mind reading, to devote even more time and attention to interpreting the intentions of others, an activity which in turn would affect the organization of their neural systems.
>
> (Hrdy 2009, 114–15)

In millennia of drought, carers looked for signs that a baby would likely survive, hence be worth the decades of investment. The signs included healthy skin tone, plumpness, vigor, and a profusion of babbling (on the last, see Chapter 3). In addition, a baby's chances of survival were hugely enhanced if she recognized carers *as* carers and responded to their attentions with joy.

Endearers endured. That may explain the unique social smile of the modern human baby. Other apes did not need it.[4]

Primed for relationship

I have indicated evolutionary factors that predispose the human baby to perceive a carer as attending. Now I want to strengthen the point using infancy research.

Psychologist Gergely Csibra argues that the human infant is *innately* disposed to perceive certain entities in certain conditions as communicating with her (Csibra 2010). He speaks of ostensive signals, meaning acts which convey to the perceiver that the actor is addressing her. For this to work in the case of a newborn baby, the acts "(1) must unambiguously specify that the infant is the addressee of a communicative act, (2) must be discriminable by newborns, and (3) must induce preferential orientation [by the newborn] towards their source" (Csibra 2010, 144). He describes three types of acts that satisfy these criteria: eye contact, parentese, and turn-taking.

Eye contact

Like the eyes of chimpanzees and bonobos, human eyes feature a strong contrast between sclera and iris, which enhances the effect of mutual gaze (Perea-Garcia et al. 2019; Kobayashi and Kohshima 2001). Human sensitivity to direct gaze exists from birth: when presented with photos of faces, newborns look more at those that seem to be looking at them (Farroni et al. 2002). As I mentioned in Chapter 1, when a schematic face seems first to gaze directly at a baby 2–5 days old, following this with a shift of the pupils left or right, the baby tends to look in the same direction (Farroni et al. 2004). On the basis of these findings, it seems likely that during mutual gaze, the baby is aware that the carer is looking—and looking means looking *at something*. I have claimed that a baby first becomes aware of herself as the *something*, and I have called the event of becoming self-aware in this looplike way a *You-I Event*.

---

4 "[O]ther great apes do not smile or laugh as they interact with others at all (that is, great apes do something similar to human smiling and laughing, but only when they are physically tickled in playful activities)" (Tomasello 2019, 54).

Parentese

Unlike eye contact, the speech signal does not specify its addressee. Babies often hear vocalizations that are directed to others. A special marker is needed for speech that is directed to them (Csibra 2010).

In all cultures, when people address an infant, they typically heighten pitch but vary it, slowing the tempo, stressing certain syllables, and often repeating a phrase. This is called *infant-directed speech*, aka *parentese* or *motherese*. Newborns prefer it. At the age of 2 days, they pay more attention to a source addressing them in it (Cooper and Aslin 1990). Evolution has primed them to welcome speech that is directed to them.

Turn-taking

Csibra asks us to imagine being in a prison cell and hearing what seem like taps on the wall. How can I determine whether it is mice or someone trying to communicate? I tap near the spot. The sound comes again, followed by a pause. I tap again and pause. The sound comes again, again followed by a pause. I don't know what meaning is being conveyed, but at least I "may confidently assume that there is a communicative intention" (Csibra 2010, 150). To determine whether a communicative intention is behind something heard or seen, one must respond and then pause, giving the possible other a chance to respond in turn. How might a newborn baby test in this way? She sucks at the nipple for a while and then pauses.

Other infant mammals suck continuously at the nipple. Uniquely, the human newborn sucks and pauses, sucks and pauses (whether fed by breast or bottle). There is no obvious physiological reason: she can breathe and swallow while sucking, and fatigue has been ruled out (Kaye and Wells 1980).

Now let us look at the carer—and in this case let us say *mother*, because the following may be instinctive with her alone. When the baby pauses during a feed, the mother tends to respond by jiggling her (or if a bottle is used, by jiggling it). During the first 2 weeks, mothers learn that when they jiggle briefly and stop, the baby will likely start sucking again. Summarizing an experiment, Kenneth Kaye writes:

> The rule 'you end your turn and I'll start mine' was being learned by the infants as well as by the mothers …. The learning in this case seems to consist in heightening the frequency of certain interactive sequences which occur naturally with some probability and then are selected by the dyad-system.
>
> (Kaye 1977, 108)

Like tapping on the prison wall and pausing, the uniquely human pause in sucking makes room for another's response. The baby has an inborn tendency to pause, and because the mother then jiggles her, the baby learns to expect the jiggle.

Nobuo Masataka has suggested a transition from such turn-taking to *protoconversation* (described in the next chapter). He conducted a jiggling experiment that included 2-month-olds:

> During interaction with the caregiver after birth, perceptual abilities develop in the infant that enable precise estimation of the length of time after ceasing a burst of sucking until the probable occurrence of jiggling. The length of time is determined by the infant's recent experiences with the caregiver. After stopping their bursts, infants learn to wait for the jiggling. If caregivers remain unresponsive, infants then coo.
>
> (Masataka 2003, 59)

Masataka elaborates: the lack of a jiggling response amounts to violation of an interactional rule. This leads to a new behavior by the infant: cooing. In return, the infant gets a vocal response from the mother. The pattern of taking turns is liberated from the context of feeding. "[T]he formation of a proto-conversational framework is achieved between infant and caregiver. With this achievement, the infant begins developing the ability to produce truly speech-like vocalizations …." (Masataka 2003, 63).

Reciprocal attention by touch

In a recent study of 72 mother-infant dyads 4–6 months old, researchers were able to isolate the effect of affectionate touch (Nguyen et al. 2021). During face-to-face play including eye contact, brain scans showed synchrony between activations in the mother's prefrontal cortex (PFC) and those in her infant's. This was expected. More surprising, however, was the fact that neural synchrony also occurred (although not as strongly) when the mother held the baby in her lap while they watched a video, the baby facing away from her. Furthermore, when they sat in separate seats beside each other and watched the video (hence without physical contact), neural synchrony declined still further. "Activation in the PFC is associated with the detection of communicative signals directed toward the self, mentalizing, and reward" (Nguyen et al. 2021, 5). Therefore, the findings suggest that in the absence of visual contact, just holding a baby can make the baby feel attended to.

There is also cross-cultural evidence. To become self-aware, infants do not need as much face-to-face attending as they usually get in the West. For example, in the rural Nso culture of Cameroon, researchers found *some* social smiling and frontal interaction at the age of 3 months, but a lot less than in a German city (Wörmann et al. 2012). Instead, the Nso mothers use more bodily contact; their vocalizations while holding the infant tend to be musical and repetitive, frequently synchronized with rhythmic bouncing (Kärtner et al. 2010). That too is a kind of attending, even without the sharp focus of a gaze.

Yet what about children who never experience another's gaze? Here is an example from the work of Ann Bigelow:

> The blind baby who remains turned away from the parent may move the hands excitedly upon hearing the mother's voice and become immobile upon hearing a stranger's voice .... These cues are often minute and difficult to detect initially .... This was illustrated for me on one particular visit to the mother of a blind child about 6 weeks of age. The mother was distressed at her baby's unresponsiveness and passivity, and she questioned whether he had other disabilities in addition to blindness. The baby was indeed inactive and appeared listless. I asked the mother to interact with her child in a way she especially enjoyed. After some hesitation, she took her baby in her arms and rolled gently back and forth on the bed talking softly to him as she repeatedly kissed him on one cheek and then the other. After a few minutes, I asked her to stop in mid-roll. She did, and the baby, who had been inactive during this procedure, slowly turned the other cheek. To the mother's delight, he showed anticipation of the coming kiss and knowledge of their intimate ritual.
>
> (Bigelow 1995, 331)

Summary

Our species has evolved in such a way that a baby is equipped to recognize a communicative partner from early in life. There is no evidence for Buber's concept of an "inborn You" (1995, 27–28), but there *is* evidence for an inborn readiness to perceive a person attending.

The ostensive signals often occur together: the mother looks into the child's eyes, starts playing with her, and calls her name in parentese. "Flooding infants with all these stimuli concurrently ... helps them to recognize the presence of a communicative intention" (Csibra 2010, 153). But what end is served by the baby's receptivity to this intention? Csibra thinks the ostensive signals alert the infant that useful information is about to be delivered. His examples of such information date to the 9th month or later, when carer and baby start drawing each other's attention to things—for instance, by pointing. We have seen, however, that the ostensive signals get responses from the infant within days of birth, and are received a few months later with smiles and coos. Is no informational content being communicated then? I hold that a very definite content is being communicated from carer to infant. It is the content *You!*

3

Becoming I through a You

In Chapter 1, I argued that a carer's attention makes a baby aware of herself. In Chapter 2, I showed the evolutionary background. In this chapter we will see how the carer's responses make the baby aware of herself as an embodied agent; how a deeper sense of self can develop when carers attune to the baby's feelings; and how self-continuity is maintained.

Protoconversation

"At the age of two to three months," writes Daniel Stern, infants "seem to approach interpersonal relatedness with an organizing perspective that makes it feel as if there is now an integrated sense of themselves as distinct and coherent bodies, with … a sense of other people as distinct and separate interactants" (Stern 1985, 69). Philippe Rochat calls the change a "second birth of the infant" (Rochat 2001, 180).

The impression that the 2- or 3-month-old has a sense of self is due, in part, to the ways she interacts with the carer, for these often resemble conversations. The baby makes lip- and tongue-movements like the ones that occur in speech. Smiles, vocalizations, and arm movements occur together in patterns like those in conversation. Also, the emotions expressed by the carer and infant seem related in the manner of address and response. The interaction occurs in turns, with little overlap. Taking these features together, researchers refer to such exchanges as *protoconversations* (Reddy 2008, 72).[1]

When Colwyn Trevarthen included turn-taking as part of protoconversation (1977), he aroused debate. It was suggested that the carer might be

---

1 For a video, see EDU Korat. Trevarthen protoconversations. https://www.youtube.com/watch?v=P-D5mkYx5eQ

DOI: 10.4324/9781003543275-4

inserting her responses during random pauses in the baby's action, giving herself the illusion of conversation. As a test, one might simply ask the carer to restrain herself and see if the baby continues to behave as before. Accordingly, the still-face experiment was devised: during playful interaction, the carer switches to a neutral expression and says nothing. If the baby's behavior before the switch was random, the change should have no effect. In fact, babies *are* affected: from the age of 2 months, they typically avert their eyes and show distress (Tronick 1989). However, they sometimes try to restart the exchange by vocalizing or smiling (Bigelow and Power 2016).

Embodiment and agency

On becoming aware of myself as the target of your attending, I-the-baby discover that my self includes a body. The principle is simple: when you focus on me, whatever I sense to be included in your focal center counts for me as me.

Consider, for example, the social smile. By 2 months, the sound or sight of you-the-carer evokes a smile from me (I have inherited the genes of endearers). How do I know that the orofacial sensation of smiling belongs to me? (For again: nothing in a sensation, taken by itself, suggests the existence of someone sensing it.) An answer has been proposed: Initially, I exist for myself as something you are looking at (or otherwise attending to). The *something* is located by your gaze precisely where feelings and sensations are being felt (namely, in the organism). In the case of the social smile, the feeling is joy, accompanied by a sensation in the facial muscles. Both the joy and the sensation are recognized by me as mine, because I perceive them to be included in what you are attending to.

At first, the social smile may happen without a prior decision to smile—hence without a sense of agency. How might it become deliberate? If your smile often follows mine, I perceive this as a response. To get the response again, I need only repeat what I am and have been doing. Your new response brings about an awareness of myself as agent (Terrace et al. 2022).

Two-month-olds understand that they can influence carers. We have evidence from the still-face experiments described above: the babies sometimes try to restart the exchange. There would be little point in trying if they were not aware of themselves as agents.

In addition to the sensations that are part of smiling, other aspects of the body become present to the baby as her own when carers include them in their act of attending to her. In the following passage from psychoanalyst Heinz Kohut, the baby's toes are recognized or reconfirmed as her own. The carer selects each toe in turn, grasping it while looking back and forth between it and the baby's eyes, and then, after the last toe, "walks" her hand toward the baby's stomach:

> "This little piggy went to market, this little piggy stayed home, this little piggy ate roast beef, this little piggy had none, and this little piggy cried wee-wee all the way home." Such games seem to rest on the setting up of slight fragmentation fears at a period when the cohesiveness of the self has not yet become totally entrenched. The tension, however, is kept in bounds (like the separation dread in the peek-a-boo game [Kleeman 1967]), and when the last toe is reached, empathic mother and child undo the fragmentation by uniting in laughter and embrace.
>
> (Kohut 1971, 118–19)

Concerning *self-continuity*: Would a baby with various carers develop various selves? The experience of *being attended to* keeps me-the-baby aware of the fact *that* I am. *What* I am in my eyes will vary according to how people relate to me, but one or two become dominant. Already from the 2nd month, an infant is more responsive to a stranger whose responses resemble the mother's in timing, intensity, and emotional quality (Bigelow and Rochat 2006). Attachment develops even when reward is scant and pain abundant (Ainsworth et al. 1972; Tronick 2009, 292).

When carers go absent

According to the logic of the account so far, if you-the-carer turn your attention away from me or leave the room, I will cease to be self-aware. From my point of view, I will cease to exist. Or do I survive your departure?

Someone may be tempted to say: "Having once been made self-aware, the baby remains so in the carer's absence." But how? We have seen no path to the self except through a carer's attending.

"Perhaps the baby hallucinates the carer attending. She has not yet learned to distinguish hallucination from reality." The idea goes back to Freud, but research shows no evidence for it. Infants are excellent reality-testers (Stern

1985, 11).[2] Also, animals have evolved to avoid hallucinating at length. Most that did so would have been eaten before reproductive age, because mental images depend on processes that are needed for perception (Kosslyn et al. 2006, Chapter 5). Dreams are another matter: I find a hidden nook for sleep or the clan posts a guard.

A close cousin to hallucination might be an "inborn virtual other" to whom the baby relates when the actual other is absent (Bråten 2009, xx). Bråten's evidence is the research I have cited on protoconversation, which shows that young babies perceive persons. But to perceive someone, you do not first need an inborn slot into which the actual person will step, nor can you interact with a slot. Infancy studies give no reason to "believe that sensitivity to social contingencies reveals an innate sense of other persons but only that it provides a starting point from which infants may learn about other persons and how they work" (Tomasello 1999, 304).

To the problem of self-awareness in the carer's absence, a simpler solution is this: the baby remembers her and hopes for her return. The memory systems of 3-month-olds are like our own in certain respects (Rovee-Collier 1997; for ways in which they differ: Gopnik 2009, Chapter 5). After seeing two puppets together for an hour per day during seven consecutive days, a 3-month-old will associate the two for at least ninety more days, even though just one of the puppets is shown in the meantime (Campanella and Rovee-Collier 2005). If association works for puppets, surely the items that are present amid a carer's frequent appearances continue to be associated with her when she is absent.

It was said above, for example, that when you-the-carer do "This little piggy," I become aware that the toes you touch are mine; in addition, they also become associated with you. When you go absent, they help keep you *present in absence*.[3] The same holds for my voice: it was part of our protoconversation, and in your absence it brings you to mind. The principle obtains for anything that was present during You-I Events: a cloth

2 Stern holds that research has nullified several psychoanalytic concepts where infancy is concerned, including the early prominence of *fantasy over reality*, as well as *undifferentiation, normal symbiosis, primary narcissism*, the *stimulus barrier*, and *part-objects* (1985, Chapter 10).
3 "To be absent is to-be-elsewhere-in-my-world …. We can in no other way explain why a mere letter from a beloved woman sensually affects her lover; all the body of the beloved is present as an absence in these lines and on this paper" (Sartre 1966, 449; and see p. 42, beginning, "I have an appointment with Pierre … .").

with your scent, the sides of the crib, the ruffling curtain, a teddy—all are *imbued* with you. "The mother or mother-substitute … is reliably present even if represented for the moment by a cot or a pram …." (Winnicott 1965, 29).

However (a big *however!*), you who are present-in-absence do not attend to me-the-baby. Lacking is the core of the self, the *something* which your attending made present. It too is a memory and a hope, but this is not nothing. Having been attended to, I cannot completely cease to exist in my awareness. I am present enough to miss you.

If you are gone for a certain length of time, a shift occurs. The you-imbued things now keep you present-in-absence *as not attending to me*, and they keep me present to myself as forgotten. I am the negative of your focal center. The *something* that came into being beneath your gaze is replaced by a void. The things are still there, but they point to an emptiness they cannot fill. This intimation of nothingness will not be forgotten.

The difference between perceiving you and not is the theme of peekaboo (played in all cultures where researchers have sought it). When you-the-carer hide behind something, pop up, hide again, and pop up again, each disappearance creates suspense, followed by joyful restoration. The same occurs when I-the-baby take the active part, repeatedly pulling the cloth off my face and laughing at the sight of you. I do this from the age of 4 months (Nomikou et al. 2017). When I put my hands on my eyes, it is not just the carer who seems to vanish; so do I. Peekaboo might be renamed *Being and Nothingness* or *Overcoming Separation*. It foregrounds my awareness of being aware.

***

In your absence, then, the memory of you and the hope for your return sustain a sense of self. Furthermore, by means of the things that remain when you go, I can gain a partial equivalent to your responses: from the 4th month, I make *effects* on them. An effect can keep me aware of myself as agent.

> Infants seem particularly inclined to shake an object that makes a noise when shaken. They scratch an object with a ridged surface, wrinkle a piece of paper, bang on a table with a solid object, separate the two parts of a breakable object, etc. It seems as if infants are looking for the maximum effects they can get from the manipulation.
>
> (Fagard et al. 2018, 23)

Effects differ from responses in important ways. The same movement on my part may elicit various responses from you-the-carer, while effects on a thing are more predictable. The predictability can be an advantage. In face-to-face play, when you-the-carer vary your responses, this demands energy from me to a degree that things do not. Nor do things get up and leave. Also, the You-I Event can reach a point of satiety, where more excitement would flood my capacity; with things I have more control.

Although effects are not responses, they can strengthen self-awareness beyond what memory and hope provide. When the red hoop wobbles into place on the spindle, it is like a confirmation. Or to take another example:

> The noise that comes from the tearing and crumpling of paper is as yet unknown to the child. He discovers (in the fifth month) the fact that he himself in tearing paper into smaller and smaller pieces has again and again the new sound-sensation, and he repeats the experiment day by day and with a strain of exertion until this connection has lost the charm of novelty .... The patience with which this occupation ... is continued with pleasure is explained by the gratification at being a cause ....
>
> (Preyer 1890, 191)

The importance of ripping paper is hard for us grownups to understand, because a piece of paper does not seem connected to awareness of our existence. The fact that we do not understand it in this way is due to a change in the structure of experience after language has been acquired (Chapter 4). From my viewpoint as a baby, however, the paper offers an ersatz You-I Event. I will repeatedly rip it until the sights and sounds have lost their novelty (their "otherness"); then I will seek a new challenge.

Why do I-the-baby explore my surroundings? Is it because all human beings by nature desire to know (Aristotle), or because of the will to power (Nietzsche)? These motives have a deeper ground: my awareness of my existence is at stake. I *must* make effects. When you-the-carer are absent, the Event is unfulfilled—I do not feel real—until an effect is made.

The deepening of the You-I Event

We saw in Chapter 1 that feelings are essential in the genesis of self-awareness. Here we are concerned with the sharing of feelings between the infant and certain carers—for example, mother, father, grandmother.

As said in Chapter 2, we perceive others' feelings—some at least—directly: "In general I do not surmise fear in him—I *see* it" (Wittgenstein 1980, §170).

Because you-the-carer see feelings in behavior, you can *mirror* my feelings back to me. Daniel Stern discusses a variant of mirroring, which he calls *affect-attunement* (1985, 138–42). When I-the-baby act on a thing or express an emotion, you may match my feeling in a different behavioral modality. For example, a 9-month-old, after accomplishing something, looks across the room at her mother and exclaims "Aaah!" The mother makes no sound in response, but she scrunches her shoulders and shimmies, *matching the intensity, joy, and duration of the "Aaah!"* Because the mother's shimmy occurs in a different modality from "Aaah!" the feeling is singled out as common to both behaviors and limited to neither. Thus it is distinguishable, with the result that one day it will be nameable.

The point suggests a solution to a problem raised by philosopher P. F. Strawson. He notes that in mastering language, we must learn two kinds of use for each "psychological predicate" (terms like *happy, sad, afraid, angry, determined, depressed*): "X's depression is something, one and the same thing, which is felt, but not observed, by X, and observed, but not felt, by others than X" (Strawson 1959, 109). How do I-the-child learn the two kinds of use for each term? In infancy, when a carer attuned to a feeling of mine, she showed me ways in which it may appear externally.

Returning to Daniel Stern: he holds that affect-attunement begins in the second half of the first year. Yet something like it occurs with younger babies too, especially when carers attune to the feelings that accompany uncontrolled behavior like sneezing, burping, almost falling, or dropping things. "Mother holds Nina (2 months) in front of her. Nina's head drops to one side, and mother responds by saying 'Opoo'" (Jonsson and Clinton 2006, 395–96).

To me-the-baby, your affect-attunements reveal a connection between us that goes deeper than behavior. It is an invisible sharing. Such connections are reserved for the few—perhaps just one—who attune to me often, day by day.

After I have begun to crawl, typically at around 8 months, the You-I Event can occur at a distance by means of affect-attunement. The self is no longer just the *something* that your gaze or voice brings to presence in reciprocal attention, rather it is now the deeper *something* to whom you attune. It is this deeper self that is threatened by the possible loss of you-the-attuner. At around 8 months begins a heightened dread of separation from you.

Toward language

From the first month of life, human babies babble, producing about 3,500 *protophones* daily: squeals, growls, "raspberries," and vowel-like sounds (Oller et al. 2021). As far as we know, other great-ape babies hardly babble at all (Hrdy and Burkart 2020; Oller et al. 2019). The reason for the difference likely has to do with another feature that distinguishes humans from them: cooperative breeding (discussed in Chapter 2). During long epochs of drought, babbling would have provided a survival advantage: babblers would have excelled in protoconversation, endearing multiple carers. Babbling would also have assured alloparents that the baby would someday speak—and therefore be worth raising.

Cries were once thought to be the main precursor to language, but "even from the first month, protophones outnumber cries by a factor of 5 to 1 or more" (Oller et al. 2021, 2). They "are the first sounds to be free of specific fixed functions," as words will be later (Oller et al. 2013, 6322). In the course of protoconversations, they come to resemble certain syllables in the carer's speech (Terrace et al., 2022, 5).

***

Yet babbling is not an attempt at speech. Of infants, Michael Tomasello writes, "Not only do they not know what adults are trying to say, they do not even know *that* adults are trying to say something. They do not even know what 'saying something' is" (2003, 19).

Why indeed should things have names? A rose unnamed would smell as sweet. From the 2nd month or earlier, a baby is aware of entities and events, but she will be a year old before she starts to use a few words and still older—18 months or so—before she grasps the principle that each thing has a name.

One reason for the delayed onset of language is that I-the-baby assume that you know me and therefore know what I want. At the age of 2 or 3 months, no doubt can arise as to whether you perceive me, because I come into being for myself as what you are attending to. I begin life in the conviction that you know me through and through.

This conviction will be shaken. An opening for doubt first appears when I start exploring things while you are absent. By making effects on them, including effects on my body, I discover aspects of myself that were not disclosed in our You-I Events (e.g., improved balance, improved coordination, excitement in the erogenous zones). Above all, *crawling* adds a new dimension to self-awareness. When I crawl (from the age of 8 months or so), there are changes in the optic array that specify me as one who is bringing the changes about (more on this in Chapter 10). I discover such aspects of myself independently of you, so I experience them to be beyond your knowledge of me. While crawling increases physical separation, it also increases separation of another kind, which consists of no longer feeling completely known by you.

As long as I believed you knew me completely, it seemed unnecessary to state my needs.[4] I had no idea that vocalizing served a purpose except as a medium of connection. Now, however, I understand that I must indicate what I want, at first by pointing.

Directing your attention to a thing by pointing narrows the gap that has developed between us. When I point, or when you do, we are attending not only to the thing, but also to each other. This is the *joint attention* mentioned in Chapter 1. As said there, we can attend simultaneously to a third thing *and* each other, as attested by reciprocal smiles or glances. When you turn your eyes toward the thing I am pointing at, I still feel attended to. I see the thing, I am aware of you seeing it, and I am aware of you aware of me seeing it. This is not just a shift from dyadic to triadic relations. Vasudevi Reddy writes: "[T]he changes in the infant's relation to the object of others' attention ... are in each case expansions and elaborations of an existing mutuality—that between self and other expanding to involve other 'topics'" (Reddy 2009, 102).

Bringing new items into You-I Events, you-the-carer talk about them. On the way to discovering that each thing has a name, it helps when you name an item I am looking at (Terrace et al. 2022, 11). It also helps if a thing named by you appears in similar but contrasting joint-attentional scenes (Tomasello 1999, 145). When I drink milk, for example, the word *mug* must be sorted out from *milk* and *drink*.[5] To adopt the names you apply to things is to stay with you while you expand and elaborate our dyad.

Thus, at last, your vocalizations are understood to have meanings. These are often unclear, to be sure, introducing new feelings of separation. Things

---

4 Toddlers "expect other people to know what they are thinking and feeling .... Thus crossing their intentions seems malign or wilfully obtuse ...." (Fonagy et al. 2007, 311).

5 *Mug, milk,* and *drink* refer to 7-year-old Helen Keller at the water pump. Her verbal development had been halted at age 18 months by a disease that made her deaf and blind (Keller 1903, 312, 316).

cry out for names and names for things. At about 18 months, a vocabulary surge begins.

What has been said so far applies to learning nouns. With verbs the matter is more complex. Children do not learn a verb in isolation, rather as part of a phrase. They learn each verb phrase separately by imitating adults. Between 1 and 3 years, they are "virtual 'imitation machines'" (Tomasello 1999, 159).

To enlarge the inventory of linguistic constructions, a child must engage in "role-reversal imitation": "[S]he must learn to use a symbol toward the adult in the same way the adult used it toward her" (Tomasello 2003, 25–28). She adopts not just a carer's words but entire manner, including intonations. "At the end of infancy and in early childhood," write Andrew Meltzoff and M. Keith Moore, "children *duplicate social roles*: behaving 'as if' they were mommy, acting from a mommy-like perspective, and expressing mommy-like desires and beliefs, even if they are not the child's own" (1994, 54; emphasis added).

The points about role-reversal imitation and the duplication of social roles will lead us to a twist in the You-I account.

4

Counterfeiting the You-I Event

A quick review: The You-I Event is typically joyful, if for no other reason than that humans have evolved to find it so. However, at stake in it for me-the-baby is awareness of my existence. I have ways to cope with the intervals between Events, busying myself with things that are associated with you. If you are gone too long, however, the you-imbued things make me present as *not* attended to. The *something* that you brought into being becomes a void. When at last you return, this intimation of nothingness is not forgotten. Starting from my 8th month, after your affect-attunements have made me aware of a deeper self, the possibility of losing you arouses *separation anxiety*. A child can quell this basic dread by playing the parts of carers toward herself in speech. It is time to present this idea in detail.

Self-talk

When alone, I-the-child can speak *as if I were you* addressing me. Or the reverse: I can speak to "you" (i.e., to me playing you in a listening mode). In either case, I play you toward myself as an actor plays a character. If I do so *convincingly*, I feel attended to.

We possess a detailed example. A group of researchers arranged with the parents of a 2-year-old named Emily to record bed- and naptime conversations with her, as well as her monologues after the parent had left the room (Nelson 1989). The recordings were made at the rate of four or five weekly for fifteen months.

Not all children engage in crib speech, and there were times when Emily fell asleep without it. Also, her language skills were advanced for her age. The ten linguists and psychologists who wrote about the tapes found various processes going on. The example presented here gives a real-time glimpse into the one that is crucial to the You-I account.

DOI: 10.4324/9781003543275-5

When Emily was 21 months old, her parents moved her to a different bedroom in preparation for the birth of her brother Stephen. After his arrival two months later, her self-talk displayed a surge of coherent narrative sequences. We focus on the session at age 23 months and 15 days (Dore 1989).

Emily's father brings her to the crib. She is crying. He talks about plans for the weekend, stressing certain words: "We're gonna go ... to Child-world ... and we're gonna buy some *dia*pers for *Ste*phen, and some *dia*pers for *Emi*ly, and we're gonna buy an *inter*com system, so that we can hear Stephen in different parts of the *house* ...." (Gerhardt 1989, 228).

After repeating the weekend plan a few times, her father tries to leave. Crying, Emily insists that she wants to "sleep in there." Naming some of her friends, he reminds her that "*big* kids, like Donny and Leslie and *Carl* and Emily and Neil, they don't cry cause they're big kids" (Dore 1989, 258). Exchanges follow about who cries and who doesn't, who is big and who isn't. Four times he reminds her that big kids don't cry. Then he leaves and Emily speaks. For several minutes she repeats the weekend plans, stressing certain syllables in the way her father had (dots indicate pauses): "on *Satur*day go Childworld ... buy *dia*pers for Emmy and *dia*pers for the baby ...."

After a few more phrases, she says:

"do ... big ... big kids like Emmy and Carl and Linda don't cry.
"*They* big kids. *They* sleep like big ... kids"

And two phrases later:

"babies can cry but—big kids like Emmy don't cry ...
"they go sleep but the *babies* cry ...
"everybod- the big kids like Emmy don't cry."

(Dore 1989, 258–59)

Three times Emily tells herself, using her father's intonation, that big kids like Emmy don't cry. She is adopting his style and words to keep herself from crying. Psychologist John Dore calls this *reenvoicing*. "Emily reenvoices the theme of buying diapers, the structural feature of listing names, and the stylistic feature of emphatic stress on names of people and objects" (Dore 1989, 245). The rhythms of certain phrases, he writes, are virtually identical to her father's. I would add: she is *playing at being him-speaking-to-her*, or in other words, she is *playing a You toward herself.*

Daniel Stern was part of the group that heard and discussed the Emily tapes once monthly for two years:

> [I]t was like watching "internalization" happen right before our eyes and ears. After father left, she appeared to be constantly under the threat of feeling alone and distressed. ... To keep herself controlled emotionally, she repeated in her soliloquy topics that had been part of the dialogue with her father. Sometimes she seemed to intone in his voice or to recreate something like the previous dialogue with him, in order to reactivate his presence and carry it with her toward the abyss of sleep.
>
> (Stern 1985, 173)

Stern here uses, in scare quotes, the psychoanalytic concept of *internalization*, which is sometimes called *introjection*. In Freud's conceptual scheme, it is a "setting up of the [love] object inside the ego" (Freud 1961, 29). Freud interprets the act as a defense against the possible loss of the carer or her love. Roy Schafer speaks of the introject as "an inner presence with which one feels in a continuous or intermittent dynamic relationship" (1968, 16). D. W. Winnicott formulates the process thus:

> Gradually, the ego-supportive environment is introjected and built into the individual's personality, so that there comes about a capacity actually to be alone. Even so, theoretically, *there is always someone present*, someone who is equated ultimately and unconsciously with the mother ....
>
> (Winnicott 1965, 35; emphasis added)

Note the contrast with the preverbal period. If you-the-carer were absent, my sense of myself could be restored somewhat when I made effects on things imbued with you, so that I got from them a partial equivalent to your responses. But there was nothing so extreme as setting you up "inside the ego." The new ability to speak enables a change. I have long been able to imitate you, but language lets me do so in fine detail. The escape from dread is the more effective, the better I conjure up your presence.

For humans, the path to self-awareness leads through another person, true or played. When talking like another toward myself, I feel attended to as if by that person—and so am recreated as a self. The catch, however, is in the *as if*. The addressee is a thin version of the self, for it is brought to presence by no true other. Nevertheless, except in certain pathologies, the resultant sense of self has the merit of being *secure* from abandonment, since I can play the parts of others at will. As for children who are deaf, they sign to themselves (Goldin-Meadow 2003, 148).

"From a psychoanalytic perspective," write Arnold Wilson and Lissa Weinstein, "the internalization of speech must help resolve some of the key developmental conflicts (such as fear of the loss of the object or loss of the object's love) with which analysts are so familiar" (Wilson and Weinstein 1990, 34). If this is correct, the desire to play the carer toward oneself, usurping the function of the You, may be an additional motive for learning to speak.[1]

Returning to Daniel Stern: As a psychoanalyst and infancy researcher in the 1980s, he was well-positioned to see the importance of the Emily tapes:

There is yet another way that the monologue can "hold on to" the presence of others. A tenet of current self-psychology is that the maintenance of the self-system is a continuous process, and that the "presence" of internalized others is a requisite of self-regulation. To put this most simply, one is very rarely all alone, mentally. ... [S]elf-regulation (even when physically all alone) occurs in the representational context of relatedness with others. Under stress or distress or anything that threatens the equilibrium of the self-system (such as separation) the internalized others are that much more activated. From this point of view, one can construe both Emily's future talk and her past talk [i.e., her self-talk about the future and the past] as types of activation of internalized others to help her self-regulate under the anxiety of separation.

(Stern 1989, 313–14)

The formation of a mental interior

When Emily says, in her father's intonation, "Big kids like Emmy don't cry," we may assume she knows that the speaker is really herself (otherwise, she is hallucinating). Yet if we follow Stern on self-regulation, she is able to control her crying and feel comforted because she suspends what she knows and hears the sentence as if it were being spoken by him—that is, as if it were coming from outside. She *pretends* that there is space

---

1 In the psychological and philosophical literature on inner speech, there is much about internalizing the language. Except for psychoanalytic thought, however, I have found nothing about internalizing the carers whose language it is!

between herself as the speaking father and herself as the hearer. In this way, she creates a *pretend space*. This space is modeled on the perceptual space in which her father would be standing if he were there.[2]

"The process of internalization is not the *transferal* of an external activity to a preexisting internal plane of consciousness; it is the process in which this internal plane is *formed*" (Leont'ev 1981, 57). It is formed in playing others toward oneself.

Pretend space is recreated in many iterations. On one side of this space is the child-as-father, -as-mother, -as-her-teacher, and so on. On the other side is the child to whom the played other is attending. The form is that of the You-I Event, but it is a counterfeit.

Mock others

The playing of others toward oneself becomes habitual to the point that it may occur automatically. I-the-adult contain internalized versions of parents, grandparents, siblings, teachers, friends, and heroes. Even when they do not speak or listen, I often feel their attention—for instance, approval or disapproval—as I go about my chores. Charles Fernyhough calls such beings *felt presences*. Speaking of the voices within, he says, "Ultimately a heard voice is something that communicates, and an entity that communicates can be represented separately from its actual utterances" (Fernyhough 2016, 229). The term *felt presences* is often used, however, to refer to hallucinated others, whereas I mean something more ordinary. In an autobiographical account, psychologist Barry Stevens expresses the ordinary phenomenon:

> In the beginning, I was one person, knowing nothing but my own experience. Then I was told things, and I became two people: the little girl who said how terrible it was that the boys had a fire going in the lot next door where they were roasting apples (which was what the women said) – and the little girl who, when the boys were called by their mothers to go to the store, ran out and tended the fire and the apples and loved doing it. So then there were two of I. One I always doing something that the other I disapproved of. Or other I said what I disapproved of. All this argument in me so much …. The most important thing is to have a career. The most important thing is to get married. The hell with everyone. Be nice to

---

2 The ideas in this chapter, and especially in this section, appeared in my "Locating the 'Inner'" (Langfur 2023).

everyone. The most important thing is sex. The most important thing is to have money in the bank. The most important thing is to have everyone like you. The most important thing is to dress well.

(Rogers and Stevens 1967, 9)

Stevens continues the inner arguments for two pages. Those who declare what is most important are the "people" she carries with her. The term *subpersonalities* is sometimes used for them (Rowan 2013), but I want to stress their function of creating a kind of self-awareness that is independent of true others. I will continue saying *internalized* or *mock* others.

Internalized others are not limited to direct acquaintances. In fifth grade, we pupils had George Washington (who could not tell a lie) and honest Abe Lincoln staring down from their portraits as we pledged allegiance to the flag. Suppose that in my adulthood a moral psychologist poses the following situation to me: "You need rags for cleaning your bathroom, and you find an American flag, so you cut it up. You're all alone and nobody will ever know. Would you feel all right about it?" (Haidt 2012, 22). But the premise is wrong: I am not all alone. I carry others with me, including Washington and Lincoln and the teachers who led us in the pledge each morning. I would feel their eyes upon me if I cut up the flag.

To take another example: on my way to the store, the thought pops into my adult head, "Don't forget to buy coffee!" I know that the words come from me, but I hear them as if addressed *to* me. Now, who said that? I as which mock other? Perhaps, at my age, it is a blend of many, a "generalized other" (Mead 1967). Hubert Hermans, originator of Dialogical Self Theory, writes of "an affectively charged, gist-like sense of an interpersonal respondent, which is based on stabilized expectancies from many past interactions" (2004, 6).

After my return from the market, I snap my fingers, "Forgot the coffee!" The roles are now reversed: it is I who speak, addressing one or more mock others, who regard me with amused or stern reproof. They are the ones for whom I put on the show of snapping my fingers.

In examples of self-talk, we do not usually find expressions like, "You're great!" or "You're an asshole!" These occur, but more typically I am talking to mock others, or one of them to me, about a third thing like coffee. Such inner speech is modeled on the You-I Event in its expanded form: the joint-attentional scene.

One speaker suffices for a conversation, if there is a listener. Or both sides may be silent while jointly attending to a third thing. The same holds for mock others. When I see a new cat in the yard, it is also seen by "them," to whom I may silently say—but need not say, since I know "they" know—"That cat's an intruder!"

The post-infancy self is a recurring product of counterfeit You-I Events. Self-talk may often seem random or superfluous—much of it is *verbal mind wandering*—but even then, it keeps its essential function. It makes me feel attended to.

Self-talk is "remarkably compelling," writes Bernard Baars, "as we can easily see by trying to stop the inner voice as long as possible. My limit for self-imposed inner silence seems to be about five seconds" (1997, 75).

The compulsive nature of self-talk is evidence of its importance. Go idle and there it will likely be. Why is it so persistent? Why can't we stop it as easily as we can stop talking aloud?

"Well, the brain just runs on," one might say. In mind wandering, however, the brain's default mode does not operate alone; its executive functions are recruited too (Christoff et al. 2009). In other words, there is method in the madness. By playing you toward myself, I persistently usurp the power that you would otherwise have to create me or not. Self-talk is compulsive because it keeps me securely aware I exist.

Self-talk restructures experience

The steady, secure, independent self-awareness that we typically enjoy as adults had its origin in a time long forgotten, when I-the-child usurped the carer's role. By around the 3rd birthday, the usurpation is permanent. Suppose that you-the-carer now re-enter the room. You can no longer appear to me in your selfhood-bestowing power. My situation has become more secure, and I won't give it up. For these reasons, self-talk *precludes* further You-Events. The self was a gift, but the self-bestowed self feels automatic and routine, like a "gift" I buy for myself. So too with *things*: they lose the fullness they had in joint-attentional Events.

The nature of space changes too. In the You-I Event of infancy you make me present to myself. You are nearer to me than my I. The distance between us is always already spanned. This ceases to be the case after self-talk has restructured experience. Space is now a mere gap between the self and others. The counterfeit inner loop has become the *subject*, while the diminished items outside it are the *objects* toward which it acts. Certain people remain important to me, but they are no longer essential to my awareness of my existence. As for inanimate things, the paper that the baby rips lies dully before the adult, who cannot understand the baby's fascination.

In the world restructured by self-talk, the question arises as to how I-the-subject am able to cross the gap between myself and objects, pick up knowledge of them, and bring it back into my inner loop. Furthermore, since I no longer need others for awareness of my own existence, I have lost the basis for my (nonetheless persistent) certainty that they have minds. Still further, the buzz of the inner conversation gives me the illusion of a consciousness contained in my head, independent of the people and things outside.

Recall too, from Chapter 1, the explanation for my post-infancy awareness of being aware. Mock others engage with me in acts of joint attention toward external things and persons. They are aware of me being aware of the things and persons. When I go to the drawer for a pair of socks, I see the drawer, but in the role of mock other I am also aware of me seeing the drawer. For much of the time, I live in a state of semi-detachment or proto-reflection. It becomes reflection when I re-enliven my playing of the other, breaking through the automaticity of habit, and entrench myself in that point of view toward me and the drawer.

This is not to say that I am always semi-detached, stuck either in proto-reflection or reflection. There are activities in which I can lose the mock others for a while, as will be seen in the chapters on work, art, conversation, and faith.

The secure self and its mock others together create the *narrative self*, whose story fills the duration between an unremembered infancy and a death that lies in a future beyond experience. Discussing minimal self-awareness in connection with narrative self-awareness, Dan Zahavi writes: "It is difficult to see how language acquisition should change and transform the very basic structure of pre-reflective self-consciousness" (Zahavi 2014, 62). Here, however, we have exposed a fundamental discontinuity between the preverbal self and the verbal, such that the original structure of consciousness is usurped by its counterfeit.

The split-off self

Self-talk is something a self does, but who is the self that does it, playing the parts of carers toward itself? It cannot be the secure self, because that is the result of the play. Is there another self in the wings who repeatedly renews self-talk?

38 Philosophy Meets the Infant

The self is split. "Ourself, behind ourself concealed— / Should startle most—."[3] It startles, for example, when I find myself saying to a colleague, "I must get this paper punished." I meant to say "published." Who said "punished"?

There is division in the self. We may partly explain it in terms of conflicting motives. Although we remember nothing of the You-I Event, there is a vague sense of lack, of a life gone gray ("Is that all there is?"). The feeling of lack indicates a *yearning* for the lost Event. The yearning is opposed by dread of fulfillment. It is dread of again depending absolutely on others who can abandon one or die.

However, dread alone would not suffice to keep the yearning from consciousness. Self-division is also explained by the structural change: I cannot stop self-talk; I cannot stop being a subject relating to objects; I cannot, by will, encounter a You. And so, a split-off self develops, yearning for something forgotten and, at the same time, dreading the dependence which fulfillment would entail.

Yearning and dreading are feelings—must they not be conscious? No, and here we have a scandal: the self, originally characterized by self-awareness, becomes partly unaware of itself. The secure self feels, thinks, acts, and lives, but concealed behind it is a split-off self, who feels different feelings, thinks different thoughts, and lives a different life—except when it breaks into awareness by inserting, for example, "punished" for "published."

We began this section with the question: "Self-talk is something a self does, but who is the self that does it?" I suggest it is the split-off self. If it can smuggle "punished" into my vocal cords, surely it is capable of playing others in speech.

Each person I encounter could make me self-aware if I were not trapped in the structure created by my own self-talk. Each is a potential but precluded You. But this is not to suggest that a true life would consist of nothing but You-I Events. Even an infant is selective. She permits only certain carers to bestow self-awareness. She can snub the babysitter by playing with things that her absent parent imbues. Yet no matter how selective the infant may be, her self-awareness depends on You-I Events with at least one person. Later it will depend on counterfeits.

3 Emily Dickinson, "One need not be a Chamber—".

The question of life's meaning

"What is the meaning of life?" When we ask this, the life we are asking about is life as we know it in a world restructured by self-talk. What *motivates* the question, however, is a hidden yearning for life as it was before the restructuring, when we were wholly given over to others from whom we received ourselves or not.

No way back

To judge from my critique of self-talk, you might think that I advocate a return to the original You-I Event. But that is impossible. I cannot talk myself into not talking to myself. The mock others inside me cannot be hushed for long, except by adepts in meditation. (But can they meditate and, at the same time, be fully given over to a flesh-and-blood person facing them?) We could organize a community that takes the Event as its goal, but our very self-consciousness about what we are attempting would probably kill the attempt. "The You meets me from grace," wrote Buber, "—through seeking it will not be found."[4]

Even if we could go back, there would be good reasons not to. Self-talk enables one to take multiple perspectives on a situation. It is needed for developing group consciousness, which Michael Tomasello calls "collective intentionality (such as an understanding of conventions and an impartial sense of fairness) ...." This begins "to emerge at around three years of age" (Tomasello 2019, 22). Since the self has become, by then, an internalized You-I Event, many a new acquaintance will be internalized too. Self-talk expands to include mock versions of new alloparents (e.g., teachers) as well as peers. They join the people we carry with us.

Internalizing new people is not easy. They present a challenge of self-continuity: How can I be the same person in relation to the mock alloparents and the mock peers too? (Recall the passage from Barry Stevens quoted above: "All this argument in me so much ....") I must reconcile the inner dialogues. Thus begins the development of a *generalized other*, that is, a *generalizing* of those mock others who stand for similar values, which typically reflect the wider culture's norms. "[T]he period from the age of three to

---

4 *Das Du begegnet mir von Gnaden—durch Suchen wird es nicht gefunden* (Buber 1995, 11).

six years … is the age at which children are beginning to self-regulate collectively and normatively—that is, in terms of *the internalized voice of the cultural group* as a whole …." (Tomasello 2019, 152–53; emphasis added).

Of the joint attention that we develop with our carers during infancy, Tomasello writes that it "arose in human evolution to facilitate coordination between individuals." In contrast, "collective intentionality arose to facilitate coordination among the members of a cultural group, even if they were unfamiliar with one another" (Tomasello 2019, 317). He presents collective intentionality as the ultimate phase in becoming human. We have seen that it depends on self-talk. The conclusion follows: to be fully human is to be a counterfeit You-I Event.

There is nothing new in the intuition that we humans are estranged from truth. It appears in various traditions, from the biblical lost paradise to the Hindu veil of maya, and from Plato's cave to Heidegger's *das Man*, the Crowd-self fleeing from nothingness. The root of our estrangement from the truth is self-talk. It is the original form of flight from nothingness. We cannot stop it for long.

"There is a goal but no way; what we call a way is mere wavering."[5]

Which is not to say that we should just give up. There are indirect paths through which the You-I Event re-enters our lives. To these we now turn.

---

5 *Es gibt ein Ziel, aber keinen Weg; was wir Weg nennen, ist Zögern.* —Franz Kafka, *Betrachtungen über Sünde, Leid, Hoffnung und den wahren Weg* (Kafka 2017, Aphorism 26).

Part 2

The You-I Event after infancy

Summing up and looking ahead: In Part 1, I showed how You-I Events make me aware that I exist, have a body, act, feel, perceive, and continue to be me. In infancy and toddlerhood, You-I Events are the norm. After that, however, they correspond to almost nothing in experience. The discrepancy is explained by the fact that I-the-child, dreading separation from those who give me being, talk with myself as if I were another. I can speak as the other while hearing as myself, or vice versa, thus gaining an illusory You-I Event. Flesh-and-blood others are no longer needed to make me self-aware. Self-talk restructures the whole of experience, precluding potential Events. Yet the yearning for these persists, stymied by a dread of reverting to absolute dependence. Because self-talk has altered the structure of experience, the yearning is unconscious.

In the chapters of Part 2, I explore the theory's power of explanation, applying it to work, love, dreams, art, and conversation.

DOI: 10.4324/9781003543275-6

5

Heidegger's hammer and the spectral You

I have argued that self-talk creates the kind of self-awareness we possess after infancy. Yet we post-infants vary greatly in how much we talk to ourselves. I confront this objection in the Appendix (Challenge 4), but I have already indicated a response: mock others and the secure self sometimes engage in silent joint attention to a thing, which includes attention to each other. Apart from that, there are derivative forms of the You-I Event which enable limited self-awareness, relieving us from the compulsion to inner speech. The derivative forms include work and art. Work is the theme of the present chapter. It is of course a huge topic, but I will limit my discussion to points where the You-I account can illuminate it.

I start with carpentry, using Heidegger's example of the hammer from §16 of *Being and Time* (1967).[1] We will later expand the discussion to include forms of labor in which the worker contributes only a fraction of the finished product or service.

There is no such thing as a hammer

Suppose that I-the-carpenter am building frames for the inner walls of an apartment. I don't normally think about the hammer while nailing. There was a time, indeed, when I first learned to use one, and then I had to look at it and think about what I was doing (where to grasp the handle, for instance). But now, while I swing it, its mode of presence is unobtrusive, freeing me to focus on the head of the nail. On the other hand, if I do single the hammer out for attention—for instance, if I put it on the seminar

---

1 I will cite the page numbers of *Sein und Zeit* (1967/1927), which also appear in the margins of the English translations, both called *Being and Time*.

DOI: 10.4324/9781003543275-7

table and say, "Consider this hammer. What are its properties?"—it appears clearly enough, but its *mode of presence* is quite different from the mode it has for me when nailing board to board. The same holds for everything I use: eyeglasses, shirt, and so on. I manage well enough with each of them as long as I do not isolate it for attention. Unobtrusive too is the sunlight pouring through the window, the floor beneath my feet, the earth as a solid support. The moment I single one of these out, its unobtrusive mode of presence slips away.

The point seems so obvious, once stated, that it is easy to miss its importance. In considering the nature of a thing, philosophers before Heidegger usually started by singling it out. The thing as it then appeared was thought to be the thing as best we could know it. In *Being and Time*, Heidegger calls this mode of presence *Vorhandenheit* (being in front of the hands, or if you will, *pat presence*). But when a piece of equipment is simply used, it is present still, though differently. How then? Well, at least it is not absent. This is a remarkable realization. Pat presence is not the only sort! About equipment like the hammer, Heidegger calls its mode of presence while in use *Zuhandenheit* (handiness). This, he says, is its *genuine* mode. What can we say about it?[2]

When we turn to examine the hammer while using it, we end up saying "Ouch!" Even brief sideways glances will not do. Is there a circumstance, then, in which I can catch sight of the genuine hammer? Yes: when it is missing or broken. While I roam the apartment in search of it, hand clenching and unclenching, I feel its connection with the frames I need to finish, with the nails and the beams, and more. It occurs to me, for instance, that if I don't get the frames done today, they will have to wait until after the weekend, and my customer won't stand for that. I can't work on the weekend—my family won't stand for that. Motivating the project of finishing the frames is the more general one of success in my profession, and the motives for this may be many, including the need to feed and protect the people I love. The hammer has its significance together *with* nails and boards, *in order to* build this or that, and *for the sake of* certain goals. All these involvements are gathered into my frustration while I search. They make up what Heidegger calls an *involvement-totality*. I want to continue making the

---

2 The following interpretation of Heidegger's hammer is adapted from Stephen Langfur, "Heidegger and the Infant," *Journal of Theoretical and Philosophical Psychology* 34 (4). Copyright © 2014 by the American Psychological Association. Reproduced with permission.

frames in order to accomplish A, and A to accomplish B, and so on. At some point, the projected chain of in-order-to's must end in a goal that is significant for its own sake, creating the relative significances of the goals and things leading up to it. "The involvement-totality itself," he writes, "goes back ultimately to a what-for in which it has *no* further involvement .... The primary 'what-for' is a for-the-sake-of-which (*Worum-willen*)" (Heidegger 1967, 84).[3]

When I simply worked with the hammer (prior to misplacing it), I lived in the involvement-totality, which Heidegger calls *the world*. It unobtrusively filled my perception of hammer and nail, as it now obtrusively fills my clenching and unclenching hand. The hammer could not be a hammer, meaning what it means, if I did not already understand the totality. I aimed at the nail, but I was also aiming through it toward (without expressly thinking of) the anticipated product, as well as my customer, my family, the weekend, and more, including, wrapped in vagueness, the primary what-for that lends significance to all.

I aim through the nail toward the primary what-for. And what is that? The carpenter may answer, "I hammer to survive." But this merely raises a further question, which can be put in various ways: Survive for what? What makes life worth living? What is the primary what-for? I seem to know the answer well enough to ply the hammer, but the moment I try to name it, it is shrouded in clouds like Olympus. Nevertheless, I surely know: otherwise, the missing hammer could not mean to me what it means as I roam the apartment, hand clenching and unclenching.

"World is that which is already previously unveiled and *from which* we return to the beings with which we have to do and among which we dwell" (Heidegger 1988, 165; emphasis added). My being, therefore, is not confined to this embodied subject, from which I dispatch rays of attention now to this, now to that. My being is stretched to include an understanding of the primary what-for, *from which* I return to use the hammer. I am not only here but also there, *da* in German—hence Heidegger's term for my being: *Dasein*, the there-being. Only coming from *there*—that is, coming from an understanding of the primary what-for—can I grasp a hammer and use it.

We ask again: What is this primary what-for? The carpenter said, "Survival." Survival forever? "Well, no, of course not, one knows one will die

3 All translations from *Sein und Zeit* (1967/1927) are mine.

someday." But this answer is hardly spoken with the kind of feeling that befits the knowledge that is being asserted. When we consider that "someday" might be the next moment, a more fitting feeling would be *dread*, aka *anxiety*. We have here, then, a piece of knowledge (I will die someday) that is detached from the mood appropriate to it. How did it come to be detached?

Heidegger answers that the Dasein flees from the dread of its death by becoming what he calls the Crowd-self (*das Man*, literally *the one*, as in "one says or does such-and-such in this situation" or "one will die someday") (1967, §27).[4] We may extend his answer as follows. The projects on offer by the Crowd (e.g., getting more wealth, security, fame, sex) can seemingly go on forever (there is always more wealth to be had, etc.). To the extent that I adopt infinitely achievable goals and become absorbed in their pursuit, I give myself the illusion of being infinite too, despite knowing better.[5] That is one way in which the knowledge that I will die becomes detached from the dread that befits it. While I skillfully nail the nail, the hammer is present in its genuineness, as is the involvement-totality, but the whole endeavor is structured as a flight from my mortal condition. My hammering is genuine but *inauthentic*.[6]

The infinite goals of the Crowd-self are projected in flight from death; the meaning of the missing hammer, felt in my empty hand, derives its force from the dread I flee. The mattering of my life reappears disguised as the mattering of the hammer. Or to vary the example, note the momentary excess of mattering when you turn the key and the car fails to start. What we feel at such a moment is our life, which is precisely what we fail to feel when we say quite calmly, "I know I will die someday."

If my Dasein did not flee from the understanding of its mortal condition, if instead it "smashed against it" (Heidegger 1967, 385), then what would be revealed? Revealed would be my existence in the light of my possibly

---

4 In translating *das Man* as the Crowd-self, I follow Thomas Sheehan.
5 Heidegger does not expressly make the point about infinitely achievable goals, but it elucidates his position. In the background is an early influence: Kierkegaard, who describes our tendency to absolutize relative ends (Kierkegaard 1960, 353, 363, 364–65, 367–68).
6 See Heidegger (1967/1927, 148 and 232): When I use a hammer understandingly—not gawking at it but simply hammering with it—my understanding is inauthentic (*uneigentlich*) but in the mode of genuineness (*Echtheit*). Also Heidegger (1988, 160).

imminent death. Revealed would be my being, experienced in contrast with my possibility of not being.

Epicurus taught that there is nothing dreadful about death. "If I am, then death is not. If death is, then I am not." Why should I dread what I can never experience? The answer is simple: I experience the possibility.

The meaning of being is what I experience when confronted with the possibility of not being. The meaning of being is elusive because the dread of not being is hard to bear and we flee from it. Heidegger thinks that Dasein has its start in this flight. It "is at first unveiled to itself in its inauthentic selfhood" (1988, 170). We begin our lives in the world that the Crowd has established. "[I]nauthenticity belongs to the essential nature of factical Dasein. Authenticity is only a modification but not a total obliteration of inauthenticity" (1988, 170).

I cannot evoke the dread that befits my condition by turning my mind toward death, for when I think of death, I do so from within the means of evasion. I cannot go to dread, but it can come to me. When it does—when I discover a lump, for instance—it overcomes the means of evasion, catching me in the throat, like the *anx-* in the word *anxiety*. But then I find distraction again—for example, in the projects of diagnosis and cure.

Self-awareness: Heidegger and the You-I account

To the question of self-awareness, Heidegger proposes a solution: because the goals that lend significances to things are mine (albeit adopted from the Crowd-self), I find my self in the hammer, the nails, the frames I am building, my customer, my family, my career—in short, in an involvement-totality. To repeat a quotation from Chapter 1:

> [I]t [the Dasein] never finds itself otherwise than in the things themselves, and in fact in those things that daily surround it .... [A]s the Dasein gives itself over immediately and passionately to the world itself, its own self is reflected to it from things.
>
> (Heidegger 1988, 159)

In the first months of a human life, there is no chain of in-order-to's. The involvement-totality is a single involvement: with a You. Heidegger speaks of Dasein's *transcendence* in the sense we have seen: Dasein is always already beyond itself in an understanding of a primary what-for, *from which* it comes back to things in their significances (1988, 161–62). According to the You-I account, transcendence occurs in reciprocal attention: as an organism, the infant is beyond sense data when it perceives a person attending, *from whom* arises an awareness of the self as what the person is attending to.

In line with the You-I account, I-the-baby should disappear from my awareness when you cease attending to me. This is prevented, as we saw in Chapter 3, because I have associated you with the things that remain when you leave. The you-imbued things keep me minimally self-aware. As we also saw, the possibility that you might not return suggests the possibility of my non-existence. In this way, nothingness enters my life. Not absolute nothingness (I cannot experience that), rather its intimation. The intimation of nothingness is a foil against which I experience—when you do return and attend to me—what it means to be. I also experience beings, but *being* is what I experience *rather than nothing*.

In the beginning is a You. A You is *a* being, not being. Aren't we entitled to ask about the *openness* in which the significance of a You becomes possible, as we did in connection with the hammer? In the case of a hammer, the openness is between my primary what-for and my present situation amid boards, hammer, and nails. In the case of a You, what is the primary what-for? What makes a You significant? Nothing beyond the You. A You is intrinsically meaningful. Its meaning is *person attending* (and there follows at once) *to me*. All further meanings will be meanings for me, but the meaning of a You is more than a meaning for me, because there is no *me* without a You. We can put the point in terms of a gift: I am a gift from a You, but the gift is its own receiver.

To be sure, by taking an evolutionary standpoint, we can account for the You in a series of steps. If we set aside other factors, organisms that want to go on living are more likely than others to reach reproductive age. Since like begets like, present-day organisms have inherited a will to live (although it can be disrupted). In the human case, given the special evolutionary background (Chapter 2), the organism's inherited will to live takes the form of an ability to recognize carers as such and engage with them. We may say: a human is born *open* to carers. Or to use a term of Heidegger's, we arrive already *thrown* into their arms. Carers make the organism aware of its existence, transforming it into an I. The openness of the baby-organism is transformed into openness between the You and the I. Within this new openness, other beings receive their meaning.

Life is not intrinsically good, nor is our specific form of it. The goodness of life, the infant's joy in the You-I Event, are products of natural selection, which results from random mutations amid environmental change. The indifference of nature's hand, however, does not detract in the least from the joy that infants take in the Event or from the yearning that we later have for it.

***

Reviewing and moving forward: A baby knows the possibility of death, but not as grownups know it. For a baby, death is the intimation of nothingness when the carer is gone a long time. The baby's dread of separation becomes plain to others after her relations with one or two carers have deepened. This *separation anxiety* typically begins in the 8th month and appears until the end of the 3rd year, by which time self-talk has eclipsed the need for a flesh-and-blood You. There persists, nonetheless, an unconscious yearning for the Event. In infancy the Event simply happened, but no longer. It has become the primary what-for—*the primary yearned-for*—hidden from us because we dread it and have fled from it into self-talk.

We have, then, two accounts of self-awareness after infancy. In one, it is produced by a counterfeit You-I Event. In the second, Heidegger's, the Dasein finds itself in the things to which it devotes itself while engaged in this or that project, adopted from the Crowd.

Both accounts are correct, but one is based on the other. Self-talk is the first form of flight from death—that is, from the possible death of the self, as intimated by the carer's absence. I evade my absolute dependence on others by playing them toward myself in speech. Since my awareness of my existence now depends on me alone, I seem immortal to myself, despite my better knowledge.

It is only after self-talk that Heidegger's account of self-awareness steps in. Playing others toward myself, I adopt their projects, which are typically those of the Crowd. I am motivated to adopt them because I unconsciously yearn for and dread the You-I Event, which re-emerges, vaguely apprehended, as the primary what-for. The Crowd's projects offer avatars of the You (a dollar, a trophy, etc.). Unlike the You, however, the avatars can be possessed. There are always more of them to be had, and so—like self-talk—my projects nourish the illusion of immortality, despite my better knowledge.

When I get absorbed in a project, *self-talk is suspended.* The project takes over its function of bestowing my sense of my existence. It can do this, we will see next, because a derivative form of the You presides over it.

Forms of a spectral You

After self-talk has restructured experience, the You-I Event occurs rarely if ever. Nor am I aware of missing it. Other people are diminished from what they were in the preverbal period, but I do not *experience* them as diminished. I assume that the others whom I now encounter are others as they basically are, just as I mistake my secure self for myself as I basically am. In the encounter with another, therefore, the possibility of a You-I Event is forgotten, hence not missed. We have seen why: self-talk has transformed me into a subject relating to objects. I cannot switch back to a different way of being, surrendering the secure self (how would I do that?). The possibility of the Event remains outside awareness.

In everyday encounters, then, a self-talker does not knowingly yearn for a You. There arises instead a yearning for something beyond everyday encounters. This yearning may find conscious expression in a vague unease, a metaphysical restlessness, as if something has gone missing ("Is that all there is?"). A certain kind of philosophical questioning—including Heidegger's about the meaning of being—is an attempt to rediscover what self-talk has precluded.

Alternatively, the missing but unmissed Yous may be *generalized* and *hypostasized* into the thought of a great invisible You, one who lives outside our realm, a You to be yearned for and dreaded, having the power to fill what is lacking and provide significance to all. The generalized You appears in various guises. It is a specter, a product of escape from reality, but because the original You was powerful, the specter is powerful too, capable of moving armies.

Faith in God will be the topic of Chapter 13. Other guises of *the spectral You* are the infinitely renewable goals of the Crowd, such as wealth, power, fame, and erotic conquest. In these cases, the spectral You is like a carer who is present-in-absence, and I am like the infant, maintaining self-awareness by making effects on the things that remain. Earning the next dollar is an effect. So is getting a promotion or a good review. These are items that can be possessed. But a You must be other; a You cannot be possessed.

During the stresses of human evolution, as said in Chapter 2, the children who survived to reproductive age were likely to be those who took joy in the You-I Event. The inherited joy and dread of the Event are concealed behind the matter-of-fact declaration, "I hammer to survive." Forgotten after self-talk, the Event continues to haunt us, reentering life distortedly through the hammer, nails, beams, and so on. When a nail is driven home—or in philosophy, when a point is driven home—there is a feeling of satisfaction, a moment of sufficiency: a spectral You, wrapped in vagueness, bestows an approving nod. Nothingness is kept at bay.

Alienated work

Most workers do not have the privilege of seeing a project through from scratch to a palpable result. They fit themselves into the projects of others, even of anonymous shareholders. Motivated by love for my family, I may adopt another's project in order to put food on the table. The project is likely geared toward conquering and possessing some avatar of the You. I play the company's boss or owner toward myself. This carer-child relation is evident in workplace pep talks, in management's setting of goals, and in employee competitions. Wanting the 9-to-5 part of my life to be meaningful, I hitch my wagon to its projects. Perhaps I have a badge or cap or uniform inscribed with the company logo. I am part of the "Acme family." A conflict of motives is set up. Talks with the mock boss may limit the quality of my presence at the family dinner. Over the factory too, and the chain store, and the office of many cubicles, mock others preside.

Can work be authentic?

Heidegger sometimes hints that basic dread can be endured—for example, by certain poets, who, to paraphrase Hölderlin, stand bare-headed under storms of God, catch the Father's ray with their own hand, and deliver it wrapped in song to the people (*Wie wenn am Feiertage....*).

We are not done, then, with the topic of work. We will take it up again in connection with insight (Chapter 7) and the making of art (Chapter 8).

6

Love and the precluded You

As with work, the topic of love is huge. Here too I will restrict my discussion to points where the You-I account can contribute.

Young love, old love

Two observations compel a critical look at the You-I account.

1 A young lover objects as follows. "In the beginning of love, I am crazy about someone. I can think of nothing else. When the phone rings, my heart skips because it might be her, and I am flattened by disappointment if it isn't. The sound of her voice is a balm to my soul. I am constantly strategizing how to see her again, or whether to write her, and what to say. When she looks into my eyes, I am lifted straight into heaven. I walk on air, showering blessings. All envy and covetousness have fled. Every blade of grass has new radiance, because it is lit from her side as well as my own. The whole of Creation is new. The hunger for the meaning of life is filled. My cup, *our* cup, runneth over. Here is a very special other. She is set apart. There is a glow from her that appears in no one else. She is not, therefore, the kind of 'diminished other' that you say we encounter in a world restructured by self-talk. On the other hand, I do not become aware of myself through her as your 'baby' does. She doesn't fit either of the structures you've proposed."
2 An older lover objects: "My partner and I have been together thirty years. When you're with someone for a long time, you've gone through many things together. One day, the things I had gone through with her and learned about her came together and crystallized, and I saw her. All my life I'd been with human beings, obviously, but it was like a revelation: this is what a human being is. It was like space becoming denser where

DOI: 10.4324/9781003543275-8

she was. A piece of space where meaning intensifies. A definiteness. It was the simple fact that she is this person, different from me, occupying her spaces, pursuing her pursuits. Suddenly it seemed marvelous and strange that she had chosen to be with me.

"The realization happened from time to time. Often it would happen when she wasn't home and I thought of her. Then it would slip away. But now it is very frequent, even in her presence. It is there with the lightest of touches, the simplest of words—the report, for example, of how well or badly she slept. She might say the same thing every morning on waking up, and it would never be boring.

"But she is not a You in the sense of your theory. Her attending doesn't make me present to myself. Sometimes because of self-talk I miss what she is saying and must ask her to repeat it. In your terms, she is a diminished other. But that's not true!"

I will address these objections during the chapter. We start with the young lovers.

Attraction

Proust's narrator "Marcel" is riding in a fast-moving carriage and notices a woman walking on the sidewalk.

I barely had time to see the young girl (*la fillette*) coming in our direction; and yet ... as soon as her individuality, a vague soul, a will unknown to me, painted itself as a tiny image, prodigiously reduced but complete, deep in her distracted gaze, immediately, in a mysterious likeness to pollen prepared for the pistils, I felt stir in me the embryo, at once vague and minuscule, of the desire not to let this girl pass without making her mind become conscious of my presence, without blocking her desires from turning toward someone else, without ensconcing myself in her reverie and capturing her heart. However, our carriage moved on .... Was it because I had only glimpsed her that I found her so pretty? Perhaps. ... [T]he charms of a person passing us are generally in direct proportion to the swiftness of the passage.

(Proust 1919, 140–41; translations from Proust are mine)

Given the speed of the carriage, hence the practical impossibility of standing face-to-face with the young woman, the motive for dread falls away.

There simply is no time for a You-I Event, no danger of facing her. Marcel's guard drops and he glimpses the You in her.

Why precisely her? Why not another woman? Or a man? Obviously, more than the You-I Event is at play. There is, for one thing, sexual desire (the pollen and pistils). Indeed, why was sex hardly mentioned in Part 1 of this book, where I discussed the first three years of life? What about the famous erogenous zones: oral, anal, and genital?

The You-I Event is not sexual. Ten years after self-talk has restructured a life, sexual desire may flow into channels precut by the forgotten Event. Nevertheless, the difference between love and sex remains clear. Despite Marcel's talk of pollen and pistils, the possibility of coitus with the young woman is scarcely felt in his description. Dominant, rather, is his feeling that she contains the secret of the universe, "the unknown," as he often calls it. It is what one would need for fulfillment. This is not the satisfaction of orgasm, which can be had independently, but rather the completion of the Event. The possibility of such fulfillment is what Marcel glimpses in her.

To deepen the understanding of attraction, we must delve into a few of life's many possible courses. A stricture by Virginia Woolf applies:

> At any rate, when a subject is highly controversial—and any question about sex is that—one cannot hope to tell the truth. One can only show how one came to hold whatever opinion one does hold. One can only give one's audience the chance of drawing their own conclusions as they observe the limitations, the prejudices, the idiosyncrasies of the speaker.
>
> (Woolf 1929, first paragraph)

To consider love in the verbal periods, I must include factors that become important after self-talk has begun. They branch off in so many possible directions that, like Woolf, I cannot aim for human universals as I did in Part 1. I am limited by my gender (male), culture (Western industrial), and biography (raised by a mother and father in a middle-class suburb of New York City in the 1940s and 1950s). I shall restrict myself to the two main heterosexual possibilities, hoping that those who do not see themselves here will find enough, nonetheless, to draw their own conclusions.

While acquiring language, girls and boys play their carers toward themselves in self-talk (Chapter 4). A time comes, however, when many boys cease to play the mother. In relation to her, that is, they cease to practice the basic technique for precluding the You-I Event. This ban will extend to all females. Likewise, many girls cease to play the father, and the ban will extend to males generally. Why?

For reasons that will soon be clear, we start with the boy. In his 2nd year, if not before, his penis takes on a special importance for him. It is a source of pride in urination and pleasure in fondling. When it goes erect, this is not an effect he wills directly, like raising an arm; rather it may rise without his willing it, or in response to his petting, as if it were an animal attached to him. "[I]t is for him," wrote Simone de Beauvoir, "at once a foreign object and himself; it is a plaything, a doll, and yet his own flesh; relatives and nurse-girls behave towards it as if it were a little person" (Beauvoir 1956, 74). "[P]rojecting free of the body, it seems like a natural little plaything, a kind of puppet" (Beauvoir 1956, 276). "[I]t is a capricious and as it were a foreign source of pleasure that is felt subjectively" (Beauvoir 1956, 74). Fondling it, the boy behaves like a You toward it, but because the result is immediately felt, it is nonetheless identified as part of him.

I said in Chapter 3 that when the carer is absent or focused elsewhere, the effects that a baby makes on inanimate things, or on his own body, can serve as a partial substitute for her responses. In this regard, his effects on the penis are remarkable. Its lack of congruence with the rest of him (an afterthought of the gods, stitched on), along with its seemingly self-willed behavior, combine to provide the impression of a distinct living thing, with which he can maintain an alternative relationship that is always accessible. (For a case study, see Kleeman 1966.)

We may assume that the more a boy prizes this somewhat alien appendage, the greater his dread that it might be taken away. Even when carers use the gentlest terms to discourage him from fondling it in public, he is likely to hear a threat.

At some time between 3 and 6 years, a boy may connect the dread of losing his penis with the observation that his mother does not have one. As a result, he no longer wants to be like her. He is deterred, therefore, from playing her toward himself. Instead, he doubles down on playing his father and other males.

In the earlier phase, when a boy did play his mother toward himself, this was symbolically equivalent to taking possession of her. But now he has stopped playing females. One might suppose that their lack of a penis would cause him to back away from them in horror. Indeed, there *is* male horror at the sight of the vulva, as expressed in the legend of Medusa: one glance at her turned a man to stone (*petra* in Greek). Medusa's petrifying power, wrote Freud, expresses a boy's reaction on first seeing that women have no penis; the lack is lavishly overcompensated by the snakes constituting her hair (Freud 1955). Yet despite the specter of Medusa in the boy's mother (and eventually in any woman), she attracts him. What makes this possible?

When the boy ceases playing his mother toward himself, he gives up, with respect to her, his technique for precluding the You-I Event. What stops him then from perceiving her as a You? Nothing stops him. He does perceive her as a You! But shouldn't a You-I Event then follow? It cannot, because he still plays males toward himself. He remains stuck in the subject-object structure. Male-to-male self-talk binds him as the rope bound Odysseus when his ship passed the Sirens. The boy's mother and all human females make up a class of beings who would enchant him to the point of losing himself, had his crewmen not strapped him to the mast.

In each girl and woman whom the boy-become-man encounters in life, the You is present, as it was for Marcel driving by. When the carriage slows— that is, when the social situation is conducive—and when I-the-male cannot diminish or neutralize a woman by any of the usual methods (discussed below), the space between myself and her becomes electric. The tension buzzes on the skin and in the air. It is hard to conceive that she might not feel it. We are accustomed to think of this space as an aberrance within our accustomed space of subject and object, which we count as the true and only space. However, because the woman appears with the magic of a You, the space between me and her, from my side at least, pervades accustomed space.

The space of attraction is related to the space of the You-I Event. The space of the Event, recall, is *distance already spanned*: you are nearer to me than my I, and at the same time you are other (for you cannot make me present to myself unless you are other). During infancy, the original space was filled with the tension of "Will she attend or not?" The tension of erotic space is like that, but with a difference. For in the meantime, experience has been restructured. Space has been split into outer and inner. Persons and things appear *either* in modified perceptual space (no longer spanned by a You) *or* in pretend space (where mock others bestow the secure self). Neither of these derivative spaces can house a You, nor can they house you who attract me. What then shall I do with you, magical one?

When I used to play my mother toward myself, it was a kind of conquest: I took possession of her in pretend space. When I stopped playing her,

I desired instead to possess her in the perceptual space of the "real" world. During boyhood, this desire was expressed in seductive, vague, but insistent behaviors toward her. Typically, the parents and the wider culture curtailed my efforts, using phrases which I interpreted as threats of castration. Alternative channels opened into which I could redirect my desire. These included school ("alma mater") and work (we will see examples in the next chapter). But note: The principal motive of the oedipal project is not sexual desire; it is desire for a You who shines before me but is out of reach.[1]

One of the alternative channels leads to women other than the mother. At the onset of puberty, the sex-drive becomes a major force. Faced with the question, "What shall I do with you, magical one?" I seek to possess you sexually. If I seduce you and feel I've "had" you, the tension of erotic space relaxes. But the You in you has slipped away. For a You is other, and an other cannot be possessed.

We are attracted to those we dare not play toward ourselves. Apart from sexual possession, men conspire to diminish the irritating You-ness of women by holding them down in alternative ways, for example, by limiting their employment opportunities, wages, and voting rights. The technique of diminishment may be simpler, however:

> If I had been able to get down and speak to the girl we passed, perhaps I would have been disillusioned by some flaw in her skin that I had not noticed from the carriage. (And then, any effort to penetrate her life would have suddenly seemed impossible to me. For beauty is a series of hypotheses that ugliness narrows by blocking the path we had already seen opening into the unknown.) Perhaps a single word she might have said, a smile, would have provided me with a key, an unexpected cipher, to read the expression of her face and movement, which would have immediately become ordinary.
>
> (Proust 1919, 140)

When a feature is viewed as "ordinary"—no longer intimating the "unknown"—otherness is diminished. A woman is reduced to a blemish or

---

1 The demotion of Freud's ideas on childhood sexuality finds concurrence in part of recent psychoanalytic thought: "Most reformulations [of the oedipus complex] have vigorously deemphasized the defining raw biological male sexuality that was so important to the Freudian drive/conflict theory" (Balsam 2010, 511).

skinniness or heaviness or an accent or a habit or her age. The clappers of a category cut her down. The depreciation of some women goes hand in hand with perception of the magic in others. Or the same woman may be simultaneously depreciated and elevated, as when Hans Castorp, infatuated with Frau Chauchat, kept reminding himself that she had lousy posture, "let every door slam behind her, rolled her bread into balls, and gnawed at the sides of her fingertips" (Mann 1924, 210). At the root is the attraction/ irritation occasioned by a You one dare not play. Marcel is not projecting a fantasy into the passing girl. From the safety of the moving carriage, he glimpses what is there. Her beauty is not added by his imagination. Rather, he is moving too fast to subtract.

Another kind of safety is afforded by social boundaries. These may act like a *frame*, helping a man to cope with a woman's magic by limiting it.[2] For example, Marcel contrives to have a dairymaid brought to his room, on the pretext of her taking a message:

> She was adorned, for me, with that charm of the unknown which would not have been added for me to a pretty girl found in those houses where they attend on one. She was neither naked nor disguised, but a true dairy-maid, one of those we imagine to be so pretty when we don't have time to approach them; she was a bit of what makes up the eternal desire, the eternal regret of life, whose double current is finally diverted, brought close to us. Double, because it concerns the unknown, a being guessed to be divine from her stature, her proportions, her indifferent gaze, her haughty calm, but on the other hand, one wants this woman to be well-specialized in her profession, allowing us to escape into that world which a particular costume makes us romantically believe to be different.
>
> (Proust 1923, 193)

Someone may claim here too that the narrator projects his ideal into the dairymaid, but this does not work—for what would the ideal consist in? What would its content be? It has no content, it is "the unknown."

According to Plato's *Meno*, we surely know in advance what will answer a question, otherwise we will not recognize the answer when we find it; yet if we already know the answer, why seek it? In Plato this paradox applies

---

2 There will be more about frames in Chapters 8 (on art) and 9 (on conversation).

to a certain kind of question, such as what beauty is, or justice. Plato's solution is that we know and do not know. We knew once but have forgotten. We forgot at birth when our souls drank from the River Lethe. Seeking is remembering.

We drank from the River Lethe when we first began to talk with ourselves. What Marcel calls *the unknown* is the forgotten You-I Event, in which one is given over to another person and receives oneself from her.

***

We have discussed the typical experience of a boy. What about that of a girl? The clitoris seems congruent with the rest of the body, no strange appendage; she has no anatomical reason to dread its loss.[3] She lacks the boy's motive to stop playing her mother toward herself. While the mother reappears to the boy with the magic of a You, she does not appear thus to the girl. In her eyes, the mother and other women do not harbor "the unknown" as they did for Marcel. Exceptions, of course, are legion. Woolf's stricture applies.

But since there is nothing in a girl's anatomy to stop her from playing either mother or father, why should she be attracted specifically to *males*? For at around age 3, her romantic interest typically turns (but perhaps this is no longer typical) from her mother to her father—and later to other men. How to explain this?

Psychoanalyst Karen Horney suggests that the turn is innate (2019). But is there a female equivalent to the magic that Marcel experienced in the carriage? If a woman occupied it instead, would each passing man appear to her as a You? Would he seem to contain "the unknown"? If women had power, would an irritating You-ness in men lead women to oppress them?

At a certain stage, the same logic sets in. To explain it, however, we do not need a feminine equivalent of castration-dread. Initially, like the boy, the girl plays both parents toward herself. When she ceases to play her father, this is typically due to *his* initiative. As a female, she too has the magic of a You for him. Although he does not initially appear to her with that magic, she yearns for a You, as every self-talker does, and so she is

---

3 Freud's notion that the girl sees herself as castrated, as if the missing penis must mean to her as significant a loss as it would mean for a boy, has been rightly trounced. See Irigaray (1985, 46–61).

receptive when he turns toward her. The point about the father as initiator comes from Nancy Chodorow (although I would replace her reference to sexuality with the nonsexual yearning for a You):

> A girl generally does turn to her father as a primary love object, and does feel hostile and rivalrous toward her mother in the process. This "change of object" may be partly a broadening of innate sexuality, and it is probably in part a reaction to her heterosexual father's behavior and feelings toward her and his preoccupation with her (hetero)sexuality.
>
> (Chodorow 1978, 150)

The girl's father, Chodorow continues, "presents himself seductively and encourages traditional feminine gender-role behavior toward him ...." (1978, 154). She responds to his special regard by playing the female toward him, toward others, and toward herself. This requires that she stop playing the roles of males. The way is then open for any boy or man to appear to her with the magic of a You, unless she finds special ways to diminish him. Note, however, that the development depends on "traditional feminine gender-role behavior," which can change within a generation (it is changing as I write). In the case of a boy, by contrast, the development depends on anatomy.

Between the counterfeit Event and the true

As a self-talking man, I dare not play a woman toward myself, for the reason stated. Therefore, every woman appears as a You unless I manage to diminish her. Her You-ness is more pronounced when she is seen from the safety of a moving automobile, but it is also present when I see her across the room. There is little danger of a You-I Event, because mock males are ever at hand. Together with me, they seek a disqualifying blemish. But suppose we fail to find one (perhaps yearning has reached a point where I prefer not to find one). Although she is just meters away, the magical woman exists in a realm from which the structure of my being excludes me. I live on a threshold between self-talk and this person who, were it not for that, would pull me into the You-I Event. Upon this threshold, love begins and flowers and bears its fruit.

The dread of abandonment motivates self-talk, but this dread can be softened by trust, which develops in the course of keeping vows (beginning, for instance, with the vow to meet tomorrow at five by the factory gate). It can easily happen, however, that your keeping of vows misleads me into believing that I have managed to rope you in, in which case your otherness fades—and with it the You in you. If you sense this, perhaps you fight. There is a pattern: the keeping of vows, a deepening of trust, the feeling of control, the other's loss of otherness, the fight, otherness restored, a new deepening of trust, and so on. For love to thrive on the threshold, dread must be softened by trust without loss of magic.

Alain Badiou writes, "Love isn't simply about two people meeting and their inward-looking relationship: it is a construction, a life that is being made, no longer from the perspective of One but from the perspective of Two" (Badiou 2009, 29). The perspective of Two is evident in the You-I Event as it is experienced during infancy. The target of the carer's perspective is experienced by the baby. This target is the original *me* with *my* perspective. From my point of view as a baby, I do not merely *take* "the perspective of Two"; I exist by virtue of it. When this perspective is elaborated and articulated as joint attention toward other items, we have what Badiou is talking about. To repeat the young lover from the start of this chapter: "Every blade of grass has new radiance, because it is lit from her side as well as my own."

We are, however, self-talkers. Mock others intervene. With the loss of the other's otherness, the perspective of Two collapses into a blended perspective. Some of my possibilities do not easily blend with yours and are excluded. These are the "unlived lines" of the body (Rilke 1965, 434; Brown 1959, 308). Then a third person comes along who arouses the unlived lines. Now *she* has the magic.

Whether we like it or not, therefore, love cannot thrive without fighting. I struggle to regain otherness in your eyes. I struggle to make you see me again in the magic I once had for you. I must be willing to risk all, and you must come to know that.

But when the hurly-burly's done, what good is the struggle if the threshold cannot be crossed? The good is this: evoked by the other's magic, as well as trust, each split-off self finds expression. It is not chiefly a matter of deliberate confessions. Meant, rather, are the revelations to which the older lover referred: "One day, the things that I had gone through with her and learned about her came together and crystallized, and I saw her." If the bond survives the revelations, it grows in strength. Space becomes denser where she is. There is depth unfathomed in the way she wears her hat.

Consider the avowal, "I love you." It follows the dynamic of the Event. It means, "I am given over to you." In the Event as it was during infancy, I was given over to a carer and received myself from her. In grownup love, if I am given over to you, I cannot take myself back: there is no self in reserve to take me back. By the argument of this book, however, the confession "I love you" will be contradicted as soon as I talk to myself. Yet when I say that I love you, I mean it. The words are spoken from within the trust that has grown between us. The contradiction is in my being.

Love thrives on the threshold between the counterfeit Event and the true. Over the years (for we are now in the region of the older lover), a thousand routines may diminish us to a point where each becomes predictable in the other's eyes, and the magic is gone. My obtuseness is evident when I cut you off while you are speaking, change the channel without asking, eat the last of the cookies—actions witnessing to my confidence that you cannot abandon me. You respond with anger, and now—all things turn against me! For all are imbued with you: the furniture, the TV show, the food on my plate. In that *all* is the world as a joint-attentional scene. It was hidden, but now it rises into view, imbued indeed: with your anger! Your otherness was not apparent during our day's routines, when we ate together or walked together, chatted or watched TV together. We were comfortable. We felt tenderness for each other. Sometimes I talked with myself and sometimes with you. Yet now I am faced with You—not a smiling carer, rather You who freeze me in my guilt.

During the day, within our routines, right up to the moment of trespass, the structure of the You-I Event was present but hidden: the world was a hidden joint-attentional scene and you were a hidden You. Beneath our easy chatter, my split-off self continued to yearn for a You, who could and should have been you. But from the time of my trespass until we are reconciled, there You are—in outraged glory.

And then we are reconciled. Our daily togetherness amid routines is again what it was, a perpetual hide-and-seek: hiding from You while seeking You. The Event will rarely happen, if ever, for the dread is great, each of us contains mock others, and we enjoy our tender routines. As the older lover said, the experience of your otherness may become constant (an increased density of presence), but I am hardly ever, if ever, drawn over the threshold on which our love has grown. I am struck by wonder, nonetheless, that you, this person, exist and have chosen to be with me.

7

The split-off self in action

This chapter is preparatory for the next, whose topic will be art. In relating the You-I account to art, the notion of a split-off self is crucial. We have, for example, the testimony of Picasso, citing Rimbaud: "I think the work of art is the product of calculations, but calculations often unknown by the artist himself .... So we must suppose, as Rimbaud said, that it is the other that calculates in us." Also: "You start a painting and it becomes something altogether different. It's strange how little the artist's will matters .... He [Rimbaud] was completely right ... when he said 'Je est un autre'" ("I is an other").[1] This *autre* is the split-off self.

I want to justify the notion of a split-off self by showing it at work. Some readers will need no demonstration, but there may be others who balk at the idea that we have feelings we do not feel, thoughts we are not aware of thinking, and that an unknown part of ourselves influences our decisions. Whatever we may think of Freud, it is to his great credit that he found a crossing to the unknown part, as exemplified in the following section.

Prehistoric fish

The dream occurred in 1975, when I was working on my doctoral dissertation. Here it is as I recorded it immediately after waking:

I am back at the time of high school. My class is visiting a museum. We are ushered into a room which mainly consists of a large pool bordered by walkways of small white tiles. A sign says "Prehistoric Fish." And there in the pool are these fish. They are between the size of shark and barracuda. Each is covered with wart-like protrusions—although larger

---

1 Dor de La Souchère, *Picasso à Antibes*, cited in Clark (2013, 10).

DOI: 10.4324/9781003543275-9

than warts, about an inch long. The waters are turbulent. The fish are fighting with a ferocity such as I have never seen. They have a peculiar way of fighting: they bite into each other's mouths and stay locked thus until one of them succeeds in forcing its teeth clear through the jaws of the other, thus taking the entire mouth. It then proceeds to consume the victim at its pleasure. I watch two fish struggle thus. I am at once fascinated and horrified. One bites through the other, and the victim swims away, blood trailing from where its mouth was, while the victor pursues for the kill. I feel I am the victim. Watching thus, I walk around the pool until, at the far end, I somehow slip and fall in. I am under the water and the fish are coming for me. I realize that I shall wake up, but then I invent that somehow I am pulled out, perhaps by someone with a boathood—rather boathook. I am dripping wet on the edge. Now I must get back to the doorway and rejoin my class. I should not have ventured so far. I edge my way back along the walkway of white tiles, which are wet and slick. Ten feet or so before safety there stands, on the pool's edge, a white refrigerator. I cling to this, trying to work my way around. While I am holding to the door it opens, suspending me above the waters. But then it swings me over into safety.

I add one more thing which I felt that morning, although it entered my written report in one word only: *fascinated*. I found something fascinating, intense, and even beautiful in the image of the two fish simultaneously biting and being bitten. There was a vicarious feeling of fulfillment, as if to say, "This is what fulfilment would be like!"

I interpreted most of the dream on the day I had it, following the technique introduced by Freud: I considered each item separately, jotting down whatever associations popped into my mind. Here they are:

1 My father once had a cabin cruiser called "The Barracuda," which he owned with his business partner. We used to go fishing on it during my high school years. (By the time of the dream he had moved on to larger boats which he owned by himself—a sign of his financial success.) One day the Barracuda had been brought to dock, and I was pinning down the canvas over the deck preparatory to our leaving. This required carefully walking along the gunwales on three sides. My father and his partner were sitting beneath me on the deck (the canvas would form a low ceiling for them) and talking. At the stern, when I was almost done, I slipped and fell through, landing between the two men. I feared my father would

rage at me for ripping the canvas ("boathood")—but instead he was concerned lest I'd hurt myself.

The place in the stern from which I had fallen corresponded in my mind to the place from which I fell at the pool in the dream.

2 The memory of falling through the canvas was followed at once by another from an earlier time, when I was 7 or so. My father's previous business partner, his first, had been my uncle, who was younger than him. Their venture had failed. I was present at a terrible argument that occurred between them in my uncle's house at the time the business collapsed. I had never heard human beings yell at one another with such ferocity. I was shocked and frightened. The image of the fishes locked in combat, mouth to mouth, each trying to bite through the mouth of the other, fits the yelling I heard that night, shout overlapping shout.

To use Freud's terminology: the *dream work* had *condensed* memories of my father with two successive business partners. I fell (as when I really did fall between my father and his partner) into the bloody fight between the fishes (as when my father and his earlier partner, my uncle, were fighting).

3 Another memory came up. A short time after the argument with my uncle, my father was engaged in building part of a beach club, which included a pool. During this period, his sister's husband died unexpectedly of a heart attack at a beach club. It was the first time anyone I knew had died. My parents took me to visit my bereaved aunt at my uncle's, and we sat in the room where the argument had taken place. She said to me, "What do you think of all this, Stevie? Pretty bloody, eh?"

4 Protrusions resembling the wart-like ones on each fish had already appeared in many of my dreams of that year, whether on a fish, a thigh, or a snow tire—or as a row of hedges. In interpreting the earlier dreams, I had understood them along the lines that Freud suggests in his study of Medusa's head (mentioned in the previous chapter). When a boy sees that a girl or woman does not have a penis, the possibility of losing his own seems realer than before. The sight of her nakedness *petrifies* him. With Medusa, as said in the previous chapter, the "lack" is lavishly overcompensated by the snakes (penises) constituting her hair. In my dream, each fish is a phallus with a mouth (vagina?), but each displays additional phalluses in the form of warts, an idea that is repeated in the multitude of

fishes occupying the pool. The dreaded act of castration occurs between the members of each struggling pair.

5 A memory arose from the age of 4: a playmate's mother baked a round white cake. She had inserted minnows into the side, their gaping heads projecting; when I saw this I ran from the place in horror.

6 The associations so far had their origins in boyhood. The next came from the year before the dream. I'd had a temporary post in the Religion department of a large university. The hall in which the pool was located brought to mind (I do not know why) the room in which the faculty members used to meet to discuss their papers. It seemed to me—and no doubt my tenuous position as the sole non-doctor contributed to the impression—that there was a lack of friendliness and trust in these discussions. I felt as if they were all out to knife each other and I'd better be careful if I *opened my mouth.*

This association was followed by an interpretation of the dream: as long as I was writing my dissertation, I could count myself as still in school. In the dream I was with my high school class, and from this secure position I could watch the ferocious infighting of the work-world, the realm of my father's success. But the completion of the thesis would mean for me the entrance into a work-world, the academic one: I would have to expose my thoughts in it, where I would face biting comments. What I had in me was to be tested. The dissertation had been slow in coming. Until the fish dream, however, I did not know the full brunt of what its completion would mean to me. The interpretation revealed that it would mean the renewal of a "prehistoric" battle: castrate or be castrated. My previous choice in life was represented in the dream's ending: to shrink away from the battle back into the sheltered life of a student. As the dream report put it, "I should not have ventured so far." The alternative to shrinking away would be to try to conquer the work-world as my father had.

I had been avoiding the battle. I was given to procrastinating (going off on sidetracks, rearranging furniture, recleaning fingernails, driving into town for this and that). It is possible to write for weeks and merely circumvent a problem when one could have bitten right through. In such matters it helps to know that dread can exist without being felt. But how can this be? The dread was felt by a self who differed from the self of which I was aware. That is the *scandal* of the unconscious. I began to understand that much of my procrastination had its motive in a feeling I did not consciously feel. By taking the unfelt feeling into account, I could rein in the tendency to putter.

A few weeks later, a new association occurred to me.

7 Using my own refrigerator, I acted out the closing scene. I realized that the place where the refrigerator stood at the pool corresponded to the place of my maternal grandmother's in her kitchen. My parents' house stood next to hers in my pubertal years. I would run to hers in the evening to watch TV (and get away from my father, who would otherwise assign me chores). I developed a phobia about the space between the houses (that I would be kidnapped, or that a ghost would grab me). I did not feel safe until I had escaped through my grandmother's dark kitchen (hence past that refrigerator) into the well-lit living room. For the rest of the evening the kitchen too would be lit, and the refrigerator became a source of puddings. In clinging to it, as I did in the dream, I was like a child at the breast.

The desire for my mother is personified in the dream, at two removes, by her mother's refrigerator. When I tried to clamber around it, I had no idea that the door might open. From being at one with my mother I am held out away from her, yet I am still part of her. She threatens to hand me over to the dangerous father, but then she relents, depositing me safely back in high school with my class. In terms of life history, achieving good grades in school, where most of the teachers were female, had somewhat satisfied oedipal yearning. But now, more than a quarter century later, I was approaching the Ph.D. Student life would have to be abandoned and a new solution found. Instead, the dream allowed me to return to high school, and I could continue sleeping.

8 For several months more I was unable to find a specific reference for the tiny white ceramic tiles that covered the walkways around the pool. Only in the final days of writing the dissertation did a memory come up. Eight years earlier, at the start of my graduate work in Philosophical Theology, I had glanced through Erwin Goodenough's book on Jewish symbols in the Greco-Roman period. It featured a mosaic from the floor of a Hellenistic synagogue, in which the image of a fish appeared against a background of small white tiles (*tesserae*). This had made an impression on me. I knew that the fish was an early Christian symbol, and the discovery of one in a synagogue mosaic brought into focus a project that was then dawning: from Judaism to answer "the crisis of faith" that vexed

the Christian seminarians in my classes. The project remained with me through my graduate work, which was guided by Stanley Romaine Hopper. He had written *The Crisis of Faith*, and had stimulated my rediscovery of Judaism. It seems fitting that the *tesserae* appeared in a dream concerned with the dissertation.

So far, the dream of the prehistoric fish has yielded a series of equivalences: my "prehistoric" mother inhabited by my "prehistoric" father = a pool inhabited by fighting fish = the academic work-world inhabited by carping professors.

Of the two fishes on which the dream focused, one represented my father, as well as my professor, and the other represented me (in the dream report I wrote, "I feel I am the victim"). I was supposed to overcome him by *opening my mouth* wider and biting through his jaws—in academia, by opening my mouth and overcoming the professors at faculty meetings. The outcome was not good for the fish with whom I identified.

Several associations present each fish as a phallus and the biting as an attempt to castrate. The horror of castration was pervasive in the dream. How then should we understand the isolated feeling that "This is what fulfilment would be like!"?

Here associations fail me. I will try to answer, but first, even without an answer we have gathered enough to see what we need to see in this chapter: the split-off self at work. The dream portrays a visit with my class to a pool of fighting fish. My father does not appear in it, nor do the other people and things that arose in the associations: his boat, the quarrel between him and his brother, my aunt's bereavement, the minnows sticking out from the rim of a cake, faculty meetings, my grandmother, my mother, the ancient mosaic, my professor, or the dissertation. Should we say, then, that these items are irrelevant? We might say so if only a few seemed to fit my situation on that night in 1975, but when all point to the same idea, which came as a useful revelation, we may say that the apparently meaningless turned out to have meaning. In the interpretation of at least some dreams, we have a path to hidden truths about waking life.

Someone may object that I inserted into the associations what I wanted or expected to find. I answer: not consciously. I simply focused on each item (i.e., each part of the dream that struck me as being an item) and allowed the associations to come. It was a form of non-purposive thinking, requiring (to echo Heidegger) a willingness not to will. Note the difference from self-talk, where speaking is an act of will. In the dream interpretation, thoughts "popped into my head," yet coalesced into a meaning.

If we agree that my dream turned out to have meaning, the following question must be taken seriously: Who was it that examined my situation vis-à-vis the doctoral work and then selected these memories, fantasies, and impressions? What wizard transmuted them into fishes, pool, and tiles? Who arranged them as a story? These are complex acts such as we would normally attribute to an artist or poet. But there was only me, who am neither, and I happened to be asleep. Who then did it? I answer: the same person as the one who, in waking hours, slips in "punished" for "published." The same one who, when writing the dissertation, kept typing Buber's title ("*Ich und Du*") as "*Ich und Due.*" Who is this person?

It is a split-off self. The interpretation of the dream shows how creative it can be.

***

Let us return to the incongruous feeling of fulfillment. Given the pervasive horror in the dream, it was odd that I found something fascinating, intense, and even beautiful in the sight of the pairs of fishes, each biting and being bitten.

I have associated the fishes with phalluses. Each fish-phallus attempts to castrate the other by biting its mouth off. Images of castration recur in the associations: the multitude of fishes, the wart-like protrusions on each, the minnows protruding from the side of the cake—in each case, many "phalluses" compensating for the lack of a phallus. Such images and associations protest too much, as if to say, "Castration is what this dream is about, so look no further!"

But remember the refrigerator. In that tagged-on incident, which occurred on the verge of waking, there is a weaker, gentler, and more sorted-out version of what was going on between the fishes. (It sometimes happens that the latent dream-thought occurs in various versions, whether within the same dream or different ones.) I wrote of the refrigerator: "In clinging to it I was like a child at the breast." Perhaps the image of the battling fishes is a cover for a primitive ("prehistoric") representation of something quite different. Perhaps each fish is not just a phallus with a mouth, but a nipple.

Feeding is an occasion for the You-I Event. To repeat Eva Simms: "Infants love to gaze at their mothers, a gaze that is one with the rhythm of breathing, sucking, and swallowing ...." (2008, 14).[2] For breastfed babies, socialization begins when the teeth start poking through at around 6 months, inciting them to bite. The babies must learn not to. Biting disrupts feeding—and the Event. Erik Erikson suggests that the mother's reactions to being bitten leave

> the general impression that once upon a time one destroyed one's unity with a maternal matrix. This earliest catastrophe ... is probably the ontogenetic contribution to the biblical saga of paradise, where the first people on earth forfeited forever the right to pluck without effort what had been put at their disposal; they bit into the forbidden apple, and made God angry.
>
> (Erikson 1963, 79)

Biting is a primitive form of taking possession. The castration fight between the fishes serves, perhaps, as a warning against the attempt to possess the You, who is the source of sustenance and selfhood. To eat the mother and still have her there—that would be fulfillment! This is what happens in sucking her milk: one eats and has her still.

Behind the oral battle of the fishes, then, might be the hidden idea of sucking the nipple. But what could be more innocent? Why should the dream-maker camouflage this? Don't young parents see the baby at the breast several times a day? Don't all of us see the same in images of Mary and baby Jesus? Yes, but we do not experience it from the baby's point of view, and this, I suggest, is the point of view in the latent thoughts of the dream. To be so radically dependent again! The thought must fill us with horror and dread, as do the battling fishes. But that would be fulfillment.

The split-off self and the insight process

If doubt remains about the creative activity of the split-off self, let the skeptic consider what it is like to have an insight. The term is used to cover various phenomena, some of which are amenable to experimental research, but I have in mind a kind of insight that is not thus amenable, at least not yet. It is the kind that occurs unexpectedly after one has reached an impasse on a

---

2 Mutual gaze while breastfeeding has been found at 3 days, although by the age of 1 month it lasts longer (Lavelli and Poli 1998).

question and left it alone for a time. Anyone who has ever wrestled with a problem or tried to create will likely have had the experience. Some of our best thoughts come in the shower. Many writers, I wager, keep a notepad by the bed. The classic example is from mathematician and scientist Henri Poincaré, who devoted an essay to the topic. Often the process begins with a period of conscious work on a question, followed by an impasse, which may cause intense dissatisfaction. "Disgusted with my failure," Poincaré writes, "I went to spend a few days at the seaside, and thought of something else. One morning, walking on the bluff, the idea came to me"—here he names his discovery, mentioning the brevity, suddenness, and immediate certainty with which it occurred (1910, 327).

The period when Poincaré "thought of something else" is known to students of insight as the stage of *incubation*. Conscious work on the problem is suspended, but work continues, unknown to the conscious self, until the idea springs ready-made into existence like full-grown Athena from the head of Zeus.

Who did the work? With regard to dreams, I have given reasons to think that the split-off self is active while we sleep and that it can be cunning, even artistic, in its choices and combinations. It also works surreptitiously in waking hours, as evinced by slips of the tongue. In the case of insight, it continues to search and think, night and day, well after mock others and their secure self have abandoned the field in "disgust."

"[W]hen motivated problem solvers cannot generate a path or strategy for solving a problem, their long-term memory systems store 'failure indices' that mark the problem as unsolved" (Davidson 2003, 163). The concept of a *failure index* comes from a paper called "Demystification of cognitive insight" (Seifert et al. 1995). The authors (tentatively) oppose the notion of unconscious work, holding instead that during the period of incubation, the thinker is alert to clues from the environment, including the ideas of colleagues, and if the right piece of the puzzle turns up, Eureka! This accounts for some insights indeed, but not all. When we walk along the cliff as Poincaré did, or board the bus as he did on another occasion, or take a shower, or nap, nothing external provides the solution—and yet, sometimes, Eureka!

By going to the seaside (no longer attacking the problem head on, no longer trying to force the matter), Poincaré acknowledges that routine approaches have not sufficed. His disgust is an opening into which a solution can dawn. When it does, he is united, for a moment, with the split-off self who has done the work.

Psychoanalysis and the You-I account

Playing others toward oneself in speech—self-talk—is the chief means for *internalizing* them, also known as *introjecting*. Psychoanalysts once believed that introjection starts in the preverbal period. "From the beginning," said Melanie Klein in 1946, "object-relations are moulded by an interaction between introjection and projection, between internal and external objects and situations" (1946, 99). But infancy research has undergone a revolution since the 1970s. One of its early representatives, Daniel Stern, opposed the uncritical application of findings from the verbal period to the preverbal.

> The infant is ... seen [in recent research] as an excellent reality-tester; reality at this stage is never distorted for defensive reasons. Further, many of the phenomena thought by psychoanalytic theory to play a crucial role in very early development, such as delusions of merger or fusion, splitting, and defensive or paranoid fantasies, are not applicable to the infancy period—that is, before the age of roughly eighteen to twenty-four months—but are conceivable only after the capacity for symbolization as evidenced by language is emerging, when infancy ends.[3]
>
> (Stern 1985, 11)

According to the You-I account, reality is distorted permanently when self-talk becomes a barrier against the You-I Event. The barrier is present in all self-talkers, even at times when the inner voice is silent. On the conscious side of it, a secure self (the subject) encounters diminished others (objects). I can be normal and happy as a self-talker, but my encounters lack the suspenseful richness of the world I knew before speech. Hidden behind the barrier is a dread-stymied yearning for that richness. Why does the yearning persist? Because of our evolutionary forebears. In times of dearth, as said in Chapter 2, those babies who took joy in the You-I Event were the ones more likely to get sufficient food and protection. The yearning persists unconsciously because it is the specifically human form of a more general *drive to live*, which is the evolutionary inheritance of all organic life.

---

3 See also Cavell (2006, 82): "We now have good reason for saying that the infant mind is acquainted with reality from the first ...."

With this point we enter the neighborhood of Freud's *life-drive*. Freud connected it primarily to the drive for reproduction, experienced as sexual desire. His assertion of a libidinal drive in the lives of small children was anathema in his day and has been strongly disputed since. John Bowlby, using ethological studies, held that a baby's need for attachment to a carer takes precedence over all other needs. Psychologist Dianna Kenny sums up his position: "Bowlby argued that the propensity for attachment is hard-wired in both animals and humans ...." He stressed separation anxiety, which he termed *primary anxiety*, and he viewed defenses as strategies to "suppress the activation and awareness of intense unmet attachment needs" (Kenny 2013, 164). Along with other post-Freudians, such as Winnicott and Ronald Fairbairn, Bowlby "removed the sexual system from the attachment system, giving primacy to the infant's emotional tie to his/her mother" (Kenny 2013, 68).

Heinz Kohut too is a neighbor to the You-I account. In the early lives of the people whose cases he presented, the interactions with the parents were minimal or destructive. They had become adults without ever reaching the stage of a strong internalization, chiefly because they had never had adequate carers to play toward themselves. Kohut's analysand starts treatment as the product of negative You-I Events. The symptoms of such negativity in adulthood may include fears of fragmentation or isolation, feelings of deadness and meaninglessness, shame, low self-esteem, and/or unrealistic grandiosity (Kohut 1971, 120–21). The analyst's initial role, on Kohut's view, is to play the part that the parents failed to play in the early years. Within the therapeutic framework, the analyst meets the patient's grandiosity and exhibitionism with approval, replicating "the gleam in the mother's eye" (Kohut 1971, 116). Also, the analyst accepts the patient's admiration, which seems overblown by adult standards, but which suits what a baby feels in relation to a carer. Kohut calls the process a "restoration of the self": the adjustment to the adult world occurs at a later stage of therapy, when the patient *internalizes* the analyst (!) (Kohut 1977, 32).

What distinguishes the You-I account is its idea of *why* attachment is important: the carer makes me-the-baby aware of my existence, in which I take joy.

Bowlby, Winnicott, Kohut, and object-relations analysts like Stephen Mitchell worked intuitively within the You-I account. If their awareness of the Event had been explicit, they would have had to face the problem of why it hardly occurs after infancy. They had the answer: *internalization*. But they did not have the question.

8

The You-I Event in art

The fictive frame

There are stories so riveting that self-talk ceases. To rivet, they must have a *fictive frame*, which differentiates between the world inside the frame and my current world. Inside are a different time and space (e.g., "Once upon a time, in a kingdom far away—"). The frame invites me to enter, leaving my world behind.

Paintings too have fictive frames (with exceptions, of which more later). I walk from the bus stop to the museum to see a new exhibit, noticing on the way that my colleague's favorite Sushi bar is gone. After finding the gallery, I begin to survey the pictures. One of them draws me in. I lose myself in the painting. For reasons we will discuss, I am able to leave behind my secure self, the product of self-talk who noticed the lack of the Sushi place.

Take almost any well-known oil painting done in the West from the 15th century through the 19th. I peep into a world that seems to extend beyond the visible part that the frame cuts off. For example, in Monet's *The Sheltered Path*, a man in the middle distance is walking on a broad dirt path, brightly lit by the sun, which stretches away from me-the-viewer. He has his back to me, and one of his arms hangs awkwardly out—perhaps he is using a cane. My concentration is aided by both the physical frame and a compositional one, which directs me toward the human figure. If the painting has drawn me in, I feel in my body the pace and the effort in his. Of course, I know all the while that I am looking at a painting, and I retain the possibility of moving to view another. I am here in the 21st century in a city museum, and yet I am also in another century, seeing the landscape and the figure from the viewpoint of Monet.

Nothing dramatic is happening in *The Sheltered* Path, nor is there the kind of narrative we expect from a novel or film. The depicted event is as ordinary

DOI: 10.4324/9781003543275-10

as my walk from the bus stop. Nevertheless, what is going on is extraordinary, if only because I am in two worlds at once and because, in one of these, my seeing aligns with Monet's. In his way of making art, Monet becomes conspicuously present—more exactly, present-in-absence—as is evident, for instance, in the play of light he has worked to bring out. He imbues the painting. His presence-in-absence is also palpable in the emphatic brush-strokes. The *made-ness* of a painting—hence the presence-in-absence of the artist—is very pronounced in this case, but it is always crucial to art. It is crucial because what occurs in the frame is a *fictive You-I Event with the artist.*

Recall that we yearn for but dread You-I Events. A fictive Event can happen in art because we know that the frame protects us from a true Event. How does the frame protect us? In the original Event, I-the-baby become self-aware through you; as soon as I exist, the distance between us has already been spanned by your attention. There is no break in this span where a frame might be inserted. Only after self-talk creates the subject (the counterfeit loop), separating it from objects (diminished others), is space de-spanned, emptied, and thereby opened for insertion of a frame. *Where a You is perceived, no frame can be, and where a frame can be, no You.*

The fictive frame secures me against potential You-I Events. I need not talk to myself to block them. I can "let myself go" (in the frame). That is, I can let the secure self go.

But self-talk doesn't just block You-I Events, it also provides an alternative self-awareness. Here too the fictive frame takes over: as said, it opens me to an Event with the artist. Monet is more *other* than my mock others, and the self he bestows will be less routine, pallid, and thin. Hence the delicious feeling of relief and anticipation on entering the gallery (or on opening a novel or when the lights go down in the cinema). The self that I will lose is the creation of my mock others. The self that I will gain is one that the artist will make.

Implied artist, implied audience

Consider what it is like to read an engaging novel. During the heyday of the New Criticism, in the mid-20th century, we were supposed to view the literary work of art as an object sufficient unto itself, regardless of an author's intentions or biography. This taboo was punctured by Wayne Booth in *The Rhetoric of Fiction*, where he pointed to *the author implied by the text.*

"Our sense of the implied author includes not only the extractable meanings but also the moral and emotional content of each bit of action and suffering …." (1983, 73–74). When we read a novel, "we are being directed all the while, by selection and emphasis and tone. Technically 'invisible', the author remains as … a hidden persuader" (Tillotson and Tillotson 2013, 7).

In *Middlemarch*, for instance, I can sense the implied author, George Eliot, directing me now to this, now to that. Consider the scene between the two sisters early in the first chapter. They are marriageable young women, orphaned eight years earlier and in the charge of an uncle. I will try to convey my sense of the implied author by putting words in George Eliot's mouth (I do not hear such words while reading; I insert them in italics to show how the author directs our thoughts).

> Early in the day Dorothea had returned from the infant school which she had set going in the village [*See, she initiates good things*], and was taking her usual place in the pretty sitting-room which divided the bedrooms of the sisters [*Picture this setup*], bent on finishing a plan for some buildings (a kind of work which she delighted in) [*Unusual work for a woman of her time*], when Celia, who had been watching her with a hesitating desire to propose something, said—"Dorothea, dear, if you don't mind—if you are not very busy—[*That's Celia's hesitation*] suppose we looked at mamma's jewels to-day, and divided them? It is exactly six months to-day since uncle gave them to you, and you have not looked at them yet." [*Note Celia's eagerness about the jewels: she has set herself a date for daring to mention them, while Dorothea has been oblivious to them.*]
>
> (Eliot 1911, 13–14)

After reading George Eliot's novels, Edward Dowden remarked that the form which most persists in the mind is not any of the characters, but "one who, if not the real George Eliot, is that second self who writes her books, and lives and speaks through them" (Dowden 1887, 240).

Booth distinguishes the implied author from the real one, who walks the dog, sorts her mail, and so on. He writes:

> Of course, the same distinction must be made between myself as reader and the often very different self who goes about paying bills, repairing leaky faucets, and failing in generosity and wisdom. It is only as I read

that I *become the self* whose beliefs must coincide with the author's. Regardless of my real beliefs and practices, I must subordinate my mind and heart to the book if I am to enjoy it to the full. The author creates, in short, an image of himself and another image of his reader; *he makes his reader*, as he makes his second self, and the most successful reading is one in which the created selves, author and reader, can find complete agreement.

(Booth 1983, 137–38; emphases added)

Booth writes that the book we reject as bad is often simply a book in whose implied reader "'we discover a person we refuse to become, a mask we refuse to put on, a role we will not play'" (1983, 138, quoting Walker Gibson 1950, 265–69).

Booth also writes, "Just think about your own self in the so-called real world, as compared with the virtual person you become as you escape into the high moralities of the implied author of *Les Misérables*" (1998, 378).

As in the exchanges between carer and infant, the implied author will not long retain her otherness as a You if she merely elicits my existing capabilities. Rather, based on an initial match, she can offer new ways of being. The only books worth reading, wrote Kafka, are those that serve as an "axe for the frozen sea inside us" (1977, 16). To be sure, the sea will often freeze again when we leave the fictive frame (i.e., when self-talk resumes). But not necessarily. *Les Misérables* can shape a life.

Within the frame, the implied author speaks to me of this and that (Dorothea, Celia, the rooms, the jewels), creating me as her implied reader, and I respond to her instructions in turn (picturing the rooms, etc.). In this respect, the author is like the carer who engages the infant in joint attention to things.

Someone may object to my comparison with the infant, reminding me that the infant makes *effects* on things, thereby maintaining self-awareness, while in art all effects are made by the artist. But a little reflection shows otherwise: the author or painter leaves gaps, and the reader must fill them to grasp what is happening. Dorothea "was taking her usual place in the pretty sitting-room ...." You cannot understand this clause without fleetingly picturing the room, and you cannot picture it without furnishing it. You may have little idea how to do so, but you must use whatever resources you possess. The picturing happens extremely fast—it is a blur—but unless you picture you have not read. George Eliot opened a gap and you filled it.

You took your turn. To read fiction is to engage in joint-attentional exchanges with an author who is present-in-absence.

Booth writes of "the full engagement that we enter when stories' implied authors hook us into their virtual worlds …. The *full engagement* is with the chooser, the molder, the shaper: an implied author" (1998, 377). He means full engagement within the fictive frame. In nonfictive life, the term applies to what happens in a You-I Event.

***

One virtue of a frame is that, even while engrossed, I am peripherally aware of its rim and can pull back. I let myself be sucked in because I know the way out (I can step away from the painting, leave the theatre, shut the book). This peripheral consciousness is latent during my absorption. I who stand on the gallery floor and enter the Monet am a complex entity, including a secure self and mock others. At first the Monet may draw me out of self-talk and into the frame, imperiously silencing my mock others. Within the frame a new self is created. After a while, however, mock others speak: "Don't hog the Monet!" They have been biding their time, waiting to overcome the novelty (otherness) of Monet.

The framed engagement with the artist provides a taste of life's original structure. That taste is the source of our enchantment and, for some of us, our addiction.

Whether we are enchanted depends, to be sure, on what occurs inside the fictive frame: something must draw me in and hold me. We will discover the source of this power if we turn from the enjoyment of art to its creation.

Making art

When the artist starts a work, the fictive frame is not empty. She has her material. Something attracts her. Cézanne goes hunting for *le motif*—why does he set up his easel with a view of this, not that? From all of Faulkner's childhood memories, why does he choose the time when his grandmother died and he and his brothers were sent from the house so it could be fumigated (Minter 1994)? And why does he modify the memory, changing fumigation to funeral rites in the parlor? Neither we nor the artist can fully answer such questions, but we can venture a few ideas.

Let me first repeat what I said about the spectral You in Chapter 5 on work. Self-talk has transformed me into a subject relating to objects.

I cannot dip down into my earlier way of being. As a subject, I am not even aware that there *was* an earlier way of being. In each of my encounters with others, therefore, the possibility of a You-I Event is forgotten. I do not think, "Oh, she's nice, but she doesn't create me *ex nihilo*." There may be, instead, a vaguer feeling of lack. Alternatively, the missing but unmissed Yous may be *generalized* and *hypostasized* into the specter of a great invisible You who fills the lack.

During much of the history of Western art, the spectral You was thought to be a god or muse breathing into the artist (in-spiring her). In recent centuries, however, art has thrived without a religious connection. It can do so because the account of the spectral You has never applied to artists. It has not applied because the artist's awareness is not limited to that of a subject aware of objects. When finding her material and working on it, the artist is accessible to the split-off self who yearns for and dreads a You in *each* encounter.

In dreams, to be sure, all of us are accessible to the split-off self, more so at least than in waking life. Recall my fish dream from Chapter 7. Was it a work of art? In a way it was for me, but that is because of the associations that underlay it, at first without my being conscious of them. In other words, the fish tale carried power for me (enough that I was moved to interpret it), and this power was due to unconscious memories, feelings, and thoughts, which the method of association brought to consciousness. But when I report the dream to you, minus the associations, it does not draw you in as an artwork would. You might feel a certain horror at the image suggesting pairs of phalluses, one in each pair attempting to bite the other off. But you have heard nothing about the quarrel between my father and his business partner, the father-son relation, the professor-student relation, and so on. Nor do the associations form an artwork when I list them as I did in Chapter 7. To compose an artwork from them, talent would be required. Strangely, though, the split-off self appears to have this talent. For, to repeat a point, who was it that examined my situation vis-à-vis the doctoral work and then selected these memories and impressions? What wizard transmuted my father, his boat, his partners, the memory of a cake decorated with minnows, the faculty meetings, the mosaic in a book on Jewish symbols, my grandmother's refrigerator, and my dissertation, into a high school visit to a pool of fishes? Who came up with the plot? These are acts such as we would indeed attribute to an artist, but, as said, there was only sleeping me. Who then did it? The split-off self.

When I say, therefore, that the artist has access to the split-off self, I mean that she has access to the same creative power that we all have when we dream. It is the power to weave associations into a tale or image. The associations are normally hidden from waking life, but (for reasons we will see) the fictive frame gives the artist access to them. When some of her associations connect with those in the split-off selves of her audience, the resulting work will resonate immediately and deeply with the latter. At the least, a feeling of significance gets through, even if we sometimes need interpreters to articulate it.

Why does the artist have access to her split-off self when awake, whereas most of us have it only in sleep? We may start with ourselves. Why do we, as sleepers, have access to it? The split in the self, I have said, consists of a barrier separating the self as a subject from the self who, in each encounter, seeks but dreads a You. This barrier relaxes during sleep. The paths from the brain to muscular action are blocked, so there is no danger that our yearnings will have results in the world. Thoughts that we do not dare to think in waking life (more exactly, not with the feelings that are bound to them) are permitted expression—not in raw form, to be sure, because they might still wake us in panic. The split-off self disguises them. "The dream is the guardian of sleep," wrote Freud (1991, Chapter 7). It is one of several guardians (Parrino and Vaudano 2018).

Now compare the artist. In one important way, she is like the sleeper whose voluntary muscles are out of action: Unconscious yearning and dread can be permitted expression because art makes nothing happen in the world outside the frame. As in dreaming, so in art: the split-off self requires an assurance of inconsequence: "What follows is mere play, it will have no practical effect." The assurance is provided by the fictive frame. What sleep is to the dreamer, the frame is to the artist. Inside it, the barrier softens. It is like a pact with the devil, as if the artist swears to her split-off self, "Nothing I do in the frame will affect anything, so there's no harm joining your powers to mine." *Je est en autre.*

Someone may object that art *can* change its audience—remember the ice axe! Yes, but let us get the levels right: at a level deeper than our accustomed world, art does have effects. The ice axe shatters the structure created by self-talk, namely the subject-object relation. The subject makes the mistake of taking the persons she encounters as being what persons basically are. But *the split-off self does not forget the You-I Event.*

It employs the same eyes as the subject but sees a different *other*. It antici-
pates, yearns for, dreads, and precludes the potential You in each encounter with a human being, as well as in encounters with you-imbued things
like mountains and apples. To the artist, the missing of the You is manifest
as a feeling of lack and potential—not the vague and general lack which
the subject feels, but a feeling of lack and potential in particular encounters (e.g., with this piece of landscape, the sunlight, the path, the walker)
or in the memory of an encounter (what it was like to be sent from the
house after grandmother's death). Because the split-off self does yearn
for the Event in particular encounters, and because the frame, by its guar-
antee of inconsequence, puts the artist in touch with her split-off self, at
least some persons or things appear as having the possibility of a fuller
presence. They appear, that is, as *insufficient*. Peering at them through a
potential frame, the artist wants to bring them to sufficiency. She may
think of what she sees as a power emanating from a person, mountain, or
apples, but the source is the power that persons once had and could have
again, and that mountains or apples once had and could have again, in the
loop of the You-I Event.

This power is what we non-artists fail to feel in particular encounters, but
it is what we unconsciously yearn for. When the artist brings forth what has
been lacking in our usual experience of the mountain, apple, or children,
the result fulfills this yearning. The frozen sea is broken—safely within
the frame. Whether the thaw continues when we leave the frame is another
question. But if art educates the emotions, as many attest, we can understand the education in this light.

As in the enjoyment of art, so its making is a joint-attentional You-I Event
within a frame. The You, in this case, is the potential (present-in-absence)
audience. The artist concentrates on what is gradually appearing in the
frame—that is, on what she feels to be potentially present in the encounter.
For Cézanne, it is something about Mont Sainte-Victoire. For Faulkner, it
is something about a character he names Caddy. But the artist is attending
to the mountain or Caddy jointly with the potential audience, namely the
potential You whose unconscious she is engaging and whose consciousness
she is changing.

To summarize: The split-off self yearns for but dreads the potential You or
the You-imbued thing. The artist is in contact with her split-off self, because
the fictive frame provides a place without consequences in the world, like

a dream. For the artist at work, and for us who view the result, dread is quelled by the frame, and a limited You-I Event can happen within it.

Someone may object, "What about political art? It attempts to change the world!" I use the word *art*, however, in the sense of an ice axe for breaking up the structure created by self-talk. When a political campaign—say, to eliminate the death penalty—is the principal motive for the work, then the particulars are such as to represent a cause defined outside the frame. There is little room for contributions from the artist's split-off self. If we take art to be an ice axe, *political art* is an oxymoron.[1]

Exceptions

The foregoing account applies to works that distinguish themselves from their surroundings by means of a frame. It does not apply to works that have no frame, for example, ceramics and architecture. As art—in my sense of the ice axe—ceramics and architecture do not frame themselves off; instead, they re-organize the surroundings (see Wallace Stevens's "Anecdote of the Jar").

Nor does the theory of the fictive frame apply to cubism or abstract painting. In them, the artist abjures the effect of two worlds, keeping to the plane of the canvas. Facing the work, I-the-viewer have no defense against You-I Events except my usual self-talk. Instead of being drawn in, I ask myself, "What is she trying to say?" On first seeing some Jackson Pollocks in 1950, critic David Sylvester thought them "incoherent nonsense, messy, uncontrollable daubs, pots of paint flung in the public's face" (Sylvester 2012, 62).

In figurative painting, by contrast, the artist's material consists of insufficiencies in which she senses a potential for fulfillment. In non-figurative works, what does she bring to fulfillment? No thing. In the very large canvases, furthermore, you can get the physical frame into view only at the cost

---

1 "Guernica" is an exception that proves the rule. It alludes to its exceptionality, and to its public nature, by eschewing color in favor of newsprint grays, blacks, and whites. Nor was Picasso alone in its making: photographer Dora Maar had a major part. Contrary to his usual practice, Picasso invited witnesses to watch him work. Also, it is done in the style of cubism, which rebels against the two-worlds effect of the fictive frame (see the Section "Exceptions" below).

of missing something vital within it. Here is the same David Sylvester after he came to appreciate Pollock:

> I think that the absence of focal points is intended to make us get into the painting in imagination, not to try and see it over there, away from us, but to enter it and explore it …. With a Pollock we create the perspectives as we move about in the painting. We are not spectators but participants, participants in its creation ….
>
> (Sylvester 2012, 63)

As to what we may experience when participating, it is like the abandon and control undergone by the artist. She abandons herself to the split-off self, but being awake, and possessing technique, she can also be in control:

> We see beyond the 'conflict and strife', the 'violent combat', to the elegance and calm and are delighted by them, but then we can see beyond the elegance and calm to the 'conflict and strife'. … [There is] the interplay in them [Pollock's paintings] of improvisation and control.
>
> (Sylvester 2012, 62)

Various factors explain why, in the early 20th century, major artists abjured the two-worlds effect: the advent of photography and reproduction; the fact that we are bombarded with framed images as our forebears never were; the consequent tendency to experience life as if through a frame, hence the dilution of the power that frames once had. There was also a Nietzsche-like revulsion against the two-worlds effect—that is, against the tendency known as *dualism*. The cubists and their successors were not content to let the viewer treat art as time-out for truth, like going to church on Sunday.

They were right. Dualism is untruth. But so is our life. Dualism is not a worldview that we may choose to adopt or not, like choosing a book from the shelf. Precisely *as* untruth, it reflects conscious life as we live it. For instance, the dualistic rift between mind and body is a truth within untruth: it derives from the gap between the counterfeit loop of self-talk ("mind") and everything external to it ("bodies"). In its stress on what is "not of this world," dualism expresses the yearning for a lost paradise, which is a distorted image of the lost Event (distorted because the dread that accompanied absolute dependence remains forgotten). As a truth within untruth, dualism cannot be canceled by fiat. Within the general dominion of self-talk, the frame retains its magic.

A note on music

Self-talk usurps the power of persons and things to make us aware of ourselves. As a result, they appear detached from us—objects to a subject (Chapter 4). Language, which refers to them, is diminished in power along with them. The word *apple* may have been learned at a time before self-talk, when it named a thing that helped keep me aware of myself, as did all things then. Post-self-talk, *apple* refers to a thing that no longer seems essential to self-awareness. I use the same word, and the apple that it names is an apple still—but the word lacks its former power, except sometimes in a fictive frame.

The notes of a melody do not refer to anything, so their power is not diminished like the power of words. When a carer speaks or sings to a baby, for the first 18 months it is mainly music the baby hears.

> If a mother sings a lullaby to her child on the first day of life, no one would expect the child to understand the lyrics; but we might reasonably deduce that the child recognizes the mother's repetition and soothing prosody – and falls asleep accordingly.
>
> (Brandt et al. 2012, 12)

Music is part of the You-I Event from birth—or even before (see the Appendix, Challenge 1). Recall the three ostensive signals that convey to the newborn baby that she is being attended to (Chapter 2). Musical aspects are present in two of them: *parentese* and rhythmic *turn-taking*. Like infant-directed song, *parentese* is spoken everywhere (Trehub et al. 1993). Babies attend especially to its musical aspects: heightened pitch with strong variations, big changes in fundamental frequency, and a slow tempo with sharp emphases. They prefer parentese even if you filter out the lexical content, leaving only the music (Fernald 1985).

As for *turn-taking*: Stephen Malloch has studied protoconversations from as early as 6 weeks, showing that the give-and-take occurs in a pulsing rhythm. In one example, which illustrates the overall experience, a mother recited a familiar nursery rhyme, then substituted tones (di-dum) for the words; in two successive instances, when she omitted a tone, her 4-month-old supplied it on the beat; in the third interval of this sequence, the child vigorously—perhaps deliberately—entered too soon by a semi-quaver, making the mother laugh (Malloch 1999).

For the baby such singing is not referential, just as music in later life is not, but it is communicative. As said, the content communicated from carer to baby is *You!* The musical aspects of the carer's speech—rhythm, pitch, timbre, and overall form—belong to that communication.

"The structure of a language is under intense selection pressure because in its reproduction from generation to generation, it must pass through a narrow bottleneck: children's minds" (Deacon 1998, 110). In the initial stages of this passage, "infants rely on a complete battery of musical infor-mation to learn speech: timbre, pitch, dynamic stress, and rhythm" (Brandt et al. 2012, 5). Rhythmic stress information, for example, is crucial for learning to distinguish segments within the vocal stream.

At around the age of 18 months, we saw in Chapter 3, the child discov-ers that things have names. She begins listening to vocal sounds for lexi-cal connections. From then on, these are the aspects of language that she mainly hears.

> However, during the first year of life, a different type of listening pre-vails. Music as an art-form may be a way of prolonging this earlier period type, when we encountered the world as a concert and sentences were merely sounds.
>
> (Brandt et al. 2012, 12)

When persons and things are diminished in power, becoming objects to me-the-subject, their names (to repeat) lose power with them. *Music is exempt from this fate*, because it does not refer. We may also think of poetry and song, in which the musical aspect of language keeps stride with the lexical. We may think of dance as well, in which the musical aspect of movement takes over from utility.

Music escapes the restructuring of experience. Ever since our carers first vocalized their care, nothing has diminished its power. Because we live in restructured experience, we require for music a dread-suspending frame. We do not enter the frame when we use a piece as background. But when we listen—or when music pulls us in—we hear it as we heard, from a time we cannot remember, the music of You-I Events. Hence the Orphic spell, the thrill in the bones. The tune that lingers in the mind and will not let go, resisting attempts to get free of it, is more deeply embedded than self-talk.

9

The You-I Event in conversation

This chapter stands under a principle stated in the previous one: Where a You is perceived, no frame can be, and where a frame can be, no You.

Attending a lecture

Phenomenologist Alfred Schutz describes listening to a lecturer:

> [W]e seem to participate immediately in the development of his stream of thought. But ... our attitude in doing so is quite different from that we adopt in turning to our own stream of thought by reflection. We catch the Other's thought in its vivid presence ... as a "Now" and not as a "Just Now." ... The fact that I can grasp the Other's stream of thought, and this means the subjectivity of the alter ego in its vivid present, whereas I can grasp my own self only by way of reflection on its past, leads us to a definition of the alter ego: the alter ego is that subjective stream of thought which can be experienced in its vivid present.
>
> (Schutz 1962, 173–74)

When one loses oneself in the lecturer's stream of thought, why is this not a You-I Event? Because a kind of frame comes into play. In an important respect, it is not like the fictive frame of Chapter 8, for it does not divide between an actual world and a make-believe one. Instead, it delimits a section of the actual world. The topic of the lecture sets parameters, beyond which we may be confident that the speaker will not stray. If the topic is the harmfulness of tobacco, we do not expect to hear a great deal about the speaker's marital problems, except as related to smoking. The frame also consists of the physical setting, the expected duration, the language, the purpose, the seating arrangement, the nature of the audience, our obligations,

DOI: 10.4324/9781003543275-11

and various special rules (e.g., should questions be reserved for the end?). These conditions apply to the entire audience, not just to me. I attend as part of that audience, anticipating a high degree of anonymity.

In the corridor, as I approach the door to the lecture hall, I am in a proto-reflective state like the one I am in when I go to the drawer for a pair of socks (Chapter 4): in the role of mock other, I am aware of myself approaching the door. I enter, take a seat, prepare my notepad, and look expectantly at the rostrum. The lecturer takes his place there, begins to speak, and now I enter the frame, participating "immediately in the development of his stream of thought." Mock others fall silent, and the lecturer takes over their role of bestowing self-awareness. He makes me present as a member of the audience. Schutz is right to say that I am immersed in the stream of his words, without reflection on myself, but reflection is not needed to keep me self-aware while the lecturer speaks. The words are perceived to be directed to the many who include me. I am among those being attended to. In entering his stream of thought, I lose myself and gain myself, albeit an anonymous we-self. My presence to myself is not the kind that an unframed You would bestow, but neither is it the proto-reflective kind that mock others bestow. The lecturer is not played by me: Within the frame, he can inform, surprise, and enthrall as no mock other can do.

Confident of receiving my audience-self, I can dare to participate immediately in the stream. However, because the frame of the lecture is erected *within* the actual world, it is more permeable than the fictive frame. Mock others interrupt with relative ease: "Isn't he forgetting the *Ding an sich*?" "How much longer?" "We're missing the Red Sox." They may even intrude to the point that I lose track.

Conversational frames

What Schutz says about listening to a lecturer is true for any act in which I comprehend another's speech: I participate immediately in the speaker's stream of thought. Such participation can be traced back to the You-I Event: To perceive the carer as attending, the baby must participate, to an extent, in what the carer is experiencing, namely her self.

Once I am able to speak, however, and have begun to talk with myself, the structure of experience changes, as we have seen. I now have a new form of self-awareness, provided by mock others attending to me. Henceforth, if I want to understand what someone is saying, I must let go of my secure self—that is, cease talking with myself. How can I do this and remain secure? Only by meeting the other in a frame.

With rare exception, conversations occur in frames. The conversational frame is composed of limits on what can be said without embarrassment. To violate them is to break the frame. In a friendship, for instance, an erotic advance would break it, resulting either in a new frame or separation. The frame of a friendship differs in scope and depth from the frame of a job interview or a police interrogation.

A very peculiar kind of conversation takes place in the psychoanalytic frame, which typically includes "the office setting, the fee, the duration of the session, the abstention from physical contact, the avoidance of gift giving, and the positions of the patient on the couch and the analyst behind the couch …." (Gabbard 2016, 6). Within this frame is a deeper one, which has the form of a contract, partly tacit, about what the therapist will and will not do, will or will not allow, what can and cannot be expected. The psychoanalytic frame is designed so that the patient may feel safe in expressing thoughts that would normally break other frames.[1]

In more ordinary conversations, I can dip into or out of the frame of our relationship, just as I can with a painting. While absorbed in the Monet, I know I am in the museum. In the conversation with a friend, I remain aware of the frame, with the result that I can easily switch between modes: I may let myself be swept along in the stream of her thought, but I can always find the rim. At any moment I can secretly pull back and talk with myself while seeming to listen. I remain, therefore, the *secure self*: secured in turn by the frame or by self-talk.

But let us now take as our example a kind of conversation which is closer to the You-I Event. I mean a conversation between friends who talk for no purpose other than that of living in their friendship. It is a mark of such conversation that ideas and bits of humor arise which neither participant knew before they were uttered. For example, X describes a sport he witnessed in France, where a man grabs the horns of a charging bull. Y says, "He's an oxymoron." Y did not think of the pun until it was spoken. It just popped out.

This phenomenon is hard to understand as long as we believe that thinking takes place inside a person and is subsequently communicated. But

---

1 The classic work is José Bleger, "Psycho-Analysis of the Psycho-Analytic Frame," reprinted in Moguillansky and Levine (2022).

what if it were otherwise? What if this kind of event, in which a thought originates between people, were thinking in its fundamental form?

To back this suggestion, let me first repeat that the basis for speech comprehension is the You-I Event: the baby participates, to an extent, in what the carer is experiencing. Second, the You-I Event is always occurring in some way. There is never a moment when I am not in relation with another person—real, mock, spectral, or absent. Winnicott once said, "There is no such thing as a baby," meaning "that whenever one finds an infant one finds maternal care ...." (1965, 38). To this we may add, "There is no such thing as a grown-up either." Therefore, we should not think of thoughts as originating inside. Of course, I can rehearse my thought in self-talk until it passes censorship, only then transmitting it aloud, but self-talk too is a form of talk with others, albeit mock.

Thought is like a leaping spark (to echo Plato's Seventh Letter), but it cannot leap without someone to leap to. Your presence (full of meaning for me, based on our mutual history) evokes my thought. Ludwig Feuerbach saw this: "Ideas originate only through communication, only out of the conversation between person and person."[2]

Thought requires at least two. If this claim still seems strange, remember, first, that each participant in a conversation is the kind of complicated self that we become after self-talk is established. This self includes the subject (mock others plus secure self) as well as the split-off self, who yearns for and dreads the You-I Event. We have seen that the split-off self is involved in making dreams and art. In sleep, the paths to action are shut, so the split-off self may find expression in a dream evoked by the yearned-for You. In art, the fictive frame provides a space of seemingly innocent play, allowing the split-off self to find expression in a world that is shared with a potential audience. So too, when a conversation is lived for its own sake, *innocent* of conscious purpose, the yearning of the split-off self finds indirect paths to consciousness. It does not do the thinking alone, but rather with the friend, whose split-off self is included. That is how ideas and humor can emerge which neither knew in advance. The same creative wizard that produces dreams in the innocence of sleep, and art within the fictive frame,

---

2 *N]ur durch Mitteilung, nur aus der Konversation des Menschen mit Menschen entspringen die Ideen.* (Feuerbach 1981, 324). Franz Rosenzweig speaks of *Sprachdenken* (thinking through speech) (Glatzer 1961, 199).

produces wit and insight in the frame that is formed by friendship, where wizards meet.

But now we must disturb this happy idyll. Perhaps the most convincing example of a thought that originates between people—the spark that requires at least two—is the faux pas. To my horror, before I know what I am doing, I find myself joking to a friend with a limp about the different lengths of the Wicked Duke's legs in a story by Thurber. I merely meant to make her laugh, but the split-off self was on the lookout for a way to take a poke at her: "I am not lame, but you are, ha! ha!" The faux pas is *faux* for the secure self, but it is a deliberate *pas* for the split-off self.

A rare instance

A conversation between friends, undertaken for its own sake, in which ideas and humor arise that are new to the participants, is not ordinarily a You-I Event. There is a frame formed by tacit expectations. And yet the *dynamic* is the same. In the Event, I become I in relation to a You; in the conversation, my thought arises in relation to you. When I suspend self-talk by means of a frame, then the You-I Event can re-emerge in the limited and safer form of a lively conversation.

Is there no chance that a You-I Event might break the frame, overcoming restructured experience? Yes. Let me give an instance.

Many years ago in Manhattan, a friend from college sat on a bench across from me on the east bank of the Hudson at twilight. He was silhouetted by the yellows, reds, and greens of New Jersey's industrial sky, which might conceivably have contributed to the trance-like state I shall describe. My friend began calmly confiding a dilemma. He faced a decision that would radically change his life. He searched for words. We entered what was for us a new kind of frame, in which we each had a role: confider and confidant.

At first, I became immersed in the stream of his thought, as in any act of listening. But then he appeared in a certain definiteness and strangeness. I mentioned this possibility in Chapter 6 on love: how one sometimes sees the beloved or thinks of her in her definiteness, in the simple but striking fact that she is different from oneself, occupying her spaces, pursuing her pursuits.

What occurred with my friend was that the definiteness, difference, strangeness, otherness persisted while he talked. I continued to be immersed in what he was saying, but because he was now so remarkably other (as if I were just then learning what *other* means), my immersion occurred in him *there*—across the new space that stretched between us. It seemed to me that I felt what it was like to be him, choosing each word, in just that intonation and with just that forward thrust of the neck, but it was not in my neck that I felt the thrust. I felt it in his neck there.[3]

This otherness of my friend was new to me, and I was drawn out of my reserve—that is, out of the self that had sat down on the bench a few minutes before and entered the frame as a confidant. I was drawn out, but given back, since his words were directed to me, here. The feeling was of being located—and this too was something new, as if I had never been located. I was no longer in two places at once: inside and outside the frame. I was *here*. Just as he was more sharply other, so I was more sharply me.

If the moment of my friend's otherness had flickered and vanished, there would have been nothing to remember. But thanks to the hesitant, searching course of his speech, I continued to feel him there and me here. His steady way of addressing me was an assurance of continuing attention. Perhaps it was this assurance that kept me there in him while receiving myself here.

It was a succession of You-I Events. As soon as I felt *me here*, I might have fixed my attention on this interesting new self (which would have dissolved), but he continued to speak, and I continued to be drawn out. The succession ended when I talked to myself—some idiotic phrase like "Hey, this is neat!" On a later occasion, the Event was broken by a voice from within saying: "This must be what Buber meant." On other occasions, when it seemed on the verge, a voice interrupted: "It's about to happen!"

If we compare this rare occurrence by the Hudson to the good conversation described in the previous section, differences are clear. In the good conversation, the frame persists. My friend does not appear in that otherness, and my self is not located through his address.

The Event by the Hudson simply happened. Such a thing cannot be achieved and is not to be sought.

Work, love, art, and conversation—are these not enough, Peggy Lee?

3 Martin Buber reported a similar experience (1971/1929, 29).

Part 3

Philosophical issues

A new theory ought to cast light on traditional problems. In this part, we shall see whether the You-I account can do so regarding questions about self-awareness, free will, objectivity, morality, racism, God, and social action.

DOI: 10.4324/9781003543275-12

10

Other accounts of self-awareness

How is self-awareness possible? I have answered with the You-I account. But might there be a more direct solution, without the need for a You? This chapter examines six alternative proposals.

Proprioception

A commonsensical proposal goes like this: "The baby senses itself in its muscles, tendons, and joints—that is, through *proprioception*."

Self-awareness is so much a part of us that we can hardly imagine what life would be like without it. But if we try to consider a muscular sensation just as it occurs, nothing about it suggests the existence of an entity sensing it. Proprioception may expand an existing self-awareness, but it cannot be its source. The same is the case for self-touch, as when one hand touches the other. The sensation is special, but it does not point beyond itself to a toucher and a touched.

Brain science: Is self-awareness innate?

In routine situations during times of good health, your brain causes you to ignore bodily sensations that result directly from your movements, thereby freeing your attention so that you can focus on sensations originating outside you. The cerebellum receives signals of any movement you are about to perform, predicts the sensations that will accompany it, and "sends inhibitory signals to other brain regions to subtract the 'expected' sensations from the 'total' sensations and thereby change the way they feel to you" (Linden 2012, 9). Bodily sensations produced by your movements are muted and ignored. In order that this may happen, however, must you not be aware of your movements, hence of yourself? Not in my usage.

DOI: 10.4324/9781003543275-13

The term *self-awareness* includes *awareness*: our very ancient forebears in the animal kingdom may have consciously engaged in the procedure that the cerebellum performs today, but we moderns are *aware* of the outcome only. This consists in sensations, without our knowing that some have been muted. Here the previous point kicks in: nothing in a sensation conveys information that a person exists who is sensing it.

To distinguish external events as such, our brains must also discount sensations that result from our movements but that could be mistaken as originating outside us. "[W]hen you watch the bird in flight, you need to be able to tell the difference between sensory changes arising from your own eye movements and sensory changes arising from the bird's motion across the sky" (Thompson 2015, 333). To discount seemingly external changes arising from *your own* eye movements, mustn't you be aware of yourself?

Here too the brain works outside awareness. The cerebellum discounts external sensations that are due to your motor actions, thus helping you determine what is happening outside you (Thompson 2015, 333–34). In the evolutionary past, any animal who could not do this was less likely to reach reproductive age than conspecifics who could. Today, the evolved cerebellar process "isn't enough to give you the feeling of being a self who is a thinker of thoughts and a doer of deeds" (Thompson 2015, 344).

Gibson's ecology of visual perception

Psychologist J. J. Gibson gives several accounts of self-awareness. Here is a summary of the most influential: Suppose there is an animal that is not yet self-aware. While it is at rest, certain things are stationary (e.g., mountains, boulders, trees, and buildings). When it gets up and moves among them, shifts occur in their visible appearances. For instance, if the animal moves toward a tree, the tree looms larger in the center of vision, while the surrounding bushes and boulders seem to stream off to the sides until they vanish. The effect of such changes in the optic array is to specify one whose movements are bringing them about. They also specify, as part of this entity, the muscles used in moving: "Visual kinesthesis goes along with muscular kinesthesis" (J. J. Gibson 2015, 175). The animal thus becomes aware of itself as a bounded entity and agent. At no point can it or need it turn "inward" to perceive itself. From its point of view, it exists strictly in connection with the external changes that specify it during locomotion. "Egoreception accompanies exteroception, like the other side of a coin" (J. J. Gibson 2015, 116).

Gibson's solution is as simple as it is elegant. Note, though, that it requires self-locomotion. It is relevant for humans once we begin to crawl, typically at around 8 months, but as said in Chapter 3, we are self-aware by *2 months*.

Defending the relevance of Gibson's solution for humans, someone may point out that a pre-crawling baby, when carried about, perceives shifts in the optic array. True, but the shifts do not single her out as one who is causing them; that is, they do not provide a sense of agency. And yet, months before crawling, the baby *is* aware of her agency. During the still-face experiment, she sometimes attempts to renew interaction; by 4 months she distinguishes between what she can reach and what she cannot. Prior to self-locomotion, how did she gain this awareness of herself as an agent? The answer does not occur in Gibson. It does occur in the You-I account (Chapter 3).

Gibson offers additional solutions, which I will treat briefly. He notes that from birth the infant can move her head and that therefore the following would apply: "[T]he world is revealed and concealed as the head moves, in ways that specify exactly how the head moves" (J. J. Gibson 2015, 118). But I do not see how the global shifts of the visual field during head movement can specify an entity perceiving them. They amount to shifts in spectacle, but there is nothing to specify the infant as an entity existing among the entities it sees. José Luis Bermúdez notes an additional objection: "All Gibson's points about the boundedness of the field of vision … can be accepted without accepting his gloss in terms of the ego being what blocks out the unperceived hemisphere" (2000, 107).

The defender of Gibson may point out that 3-day-olds adjust head positions according to optic flow. When they sit in an apparatus where fixed patterns of dots on either side of the head appear to be flowing from front to back, they lean their heads backward (Jouen 2000). Does such an adjustment evince an existing self-awareness, or else could self-awareness originate from it? Both possibilities seem unlikely. The reaction attests to an inborn connection between posture and vision. Referring to upper and lower pathways in the brain, researchers have concluded that the information from the optic flow in this case "is restricted to its visuomotor function and not accessible to the infant in the form of self-knowledge" (Bertenthal and Rose 1995, 309).[1]

Finally, Gibson holds that the self is present to itself in certain parts of the body—the nose and eyebrows, for instance—which remain visibly stable

---

1 This is not to deny that 3-day-olds might be self-aware: we do not exclude the possibility of You-I Events between mother and fetus. See the Appendix, Challenge 1.

during shifts in the optic array. But these parts cannot represent the self unless they are already known to be part of it. Otherwise, they may "provide a good reason why a subject of experience should have a very special regard for just one body, why he should think of it as unique and perhaps more important than any other," but nothing about them suggests that they are parts of their perceiver (Strawson 1959, 93).

The reflection theory

Reflection, writes philosopher Dieter Henrich, is "… a directed activity. We have to explain how reflection becomes concentrated attention on something …. I cannot concentrate on something unless there is already some awareness of it" (2003, 255). There must be, then, a form of self-awareness that is prior to reflection. What is it? It is the form that we have in everyday life. This is the form that results from self-talk. When I muddle about in the world, reassuring myself of my existence by attending to myself through the masks of others, I am not yet engaging in reflection. Rather, I am proto-reflective (Chapter 4). An act of reflection is performed when I take a mock other's position, entrench myself in it for a while, and examine its creation: my secure self muddling about.

The proto-reflective structure of self-talk was itself created in flight from the original form of self-awareness, the You-I Event.

The minimal self

Dan Zahavi preempts the Kantian challenge as to how, in the case of self-awareness, the subject can be its own object. He notes that when I am conscious of an item, there is *something it is like* to be conscious of it. There is something it is like to taste a lemon and something else that it is like to see a jacaranda. Philosophers use the term *qualia* to name such properties of experiences. What it is like to taste a lemon is not part of the lemon. It belongs to my subjectivity. In this very minimal way, without being objectified, my subjectivity is present to me (Zahavi 2014, 22).

If I examine the experience of tasting a lemon, do I detect myself in it? Zahavi says yes: "What-it-is-like-ness is properly speaking what-it-is-like-for-me-ness" (2014, 19). To be sure, there are people who claim to find no trace of themselves in the experience, but Zahavi counters that they are looking for a self that is more robust than what he means.

He favors Sartre on this point (whose French *conscience*, translated *consciousness*, is equivalent to *awareness* in the present context): "Every conscious existence exists as consciousness of existing .... This self-consciousness we ought to consider ... as *the only mode of existence which is possible for a consciousness of something*" (Sartre 1966, 13–14). That is, the awareness of anything includes self-awareness.

Sartre and Zahavi reach this conclusion after examining experience as we know it. This is not our original form of experience; it is rather experience restructured by self-talk. When I-the-adult taste a lemon, mock others are attending to me and it. The sense of self that I get from them accompanies the tasting. It *seems*, therefore, that the awareness of anything includes self-awareness. My claim has been, however, that a baby can be aware of items without being self-aware, and that she first becomes so when one of the items attends to her. Self-awareness is the outcome of a You-I Event. I-the-adult am self-aware while tasting a lemon because I have internalized the You who makes me so.

If someone objects that the self-aware tasting of a lemon has an immediacy not found in the You-I Event or its counterfeit, I reply: In reciprocal attention, as soon as the baby is aware of the attending carer, she is aware of the carer attending *to something*, which is the self. Her self-awareness is as immediate as her awareness of the carer. This holds as well for the internalized Event.

Zahavi sometimes hints at a different ground for his position that "what-it-is-like-ness is properly speaking what-it-is-like-for-me-ness."

[T]his for-me-ness of experience ... refers to the first-personal character or presence of experience, to the fact that we have a different pre-reflective acquaintance with our own ongoing experiential life than we have with the experiential life of others and vice versa.

(Zahavi 2014, 88; also 22, 24, and 28)

He is saying, I believe, that at the level of tasting a lemon, something marks the experience as mine. It is a contrast: I experience some experiences as my own and some as belonging to others. The manner of experience differs in the two cases. As said before, to know I am afraid, I need not examine my behavior, as I must in the case of my neighbor. Nevertheless, my awareness of my neighbor's fear is no less immediate than my awareness of mine (even though she may mislead me by feigning). Recall Wittgenstein: I do not surmise fear in him, I see it.

If we follow this logic: In what it is like for me to taste a lemon, the *for me* depends on my awareness of my own experience in contrast with that of others. Hence, the "first-personal character" of my experience requires awareness of others. If so, however, then we need not settle for the minimal self-awareness available in qualia. We have learned that the awareness of others, during reciprocal attention, creates a *robust* awareness of self.

The consciousness of time

In the fifth chapter of *Self-Awareness and Alterity* (1999), Dan Zahavi exposes a possible solution to the puzzle of how we can be aware of being aware. He bases it on Husserl's studies of time-consciousness.[2] A melody serves as an example. It is composed of *tones*, by which Husserl means discrete sounds, each having sensory material that lacks discernible breaks. If you hum the song "Happy birthday to you!" the sound of the hum for each syllable will count as a tone. We can only hear a melody if, while a tone is present to the sense of hearing, other tones are non-sensorily co-present as past. For example, consider Tone 1, the sound of the hum of "ha-" in the birthday song. It is present to the sense of hearing, but it is soon supplanted by Tone 2 (the hum of "-ppy"). Tone 1 has ceased to be sensorily present, but if it were to vanish entirely you would not hear a melody. While you are hearing Tone 2, Tone 1 is present non-sensorily. In Husserl's terminology, it is *retained*. When Tone 3 sounds (the hum of "birth-" in "birthday"), Tone 2 is likewise retained. Furthermore, you will not hear the melody unless the retaining of 2 includes 1-retained. On hearing Tone 3, then, what you experience is 3 (2 (1)). Such nesting of retentions preserves the tones in their sequence, enabling you to hear the musical phrase and eventually the melody (Husserl 1991, 85).

In addition to nested retentions there are anticipations, which Husserl calls *protentions*; this becomes clear if a wrong note sounds, for we feel at once that something has gone against expectation.

Given that much, Zahavi sees a possible solution to the hard part of the puzzle: "each actual phase of consciousness retains not only the just-past tones, but also the previous phase of consciousness" (Zahavi 2014, 64–65).

---

2 Husserl's explorations of time-consciousness are spread over three decades. I am aided by James Mensch's interpretation, which shapes them into a coherent theory (Mensch 2010). A version of the interpretation that follows appears in Langfur (2016).

Since retention is a form of awareness (here equivalent to *consciousness*), so the retention of retention is *awareness of awareness*. But do we in fact retain the *retaining* of Tone 1? Rather, the act of retaining vanishes behind the retained *content* (behind the retained tone, for instance). In a late text, where "each actual phase" is called a *primal impression*, Husserl writes that when one primal impression is succeeded by another, "the new one unites simultaneously with the immediately retentional transformation of the previous one .... However, the simultaneous unification is only possible as a *content-based* fusion" (2006, 82; emphasis added).[3]

This implies that while I am experiencing a temporal object such as a melody, each perceived tone is retained, but the act of hearing it is not retained.[4] The retention of retention should not be taken for awareness of being aware. The nested retentions of tones enable the experience of the melody *and* of pastness (each retained tone fading a little when the next is retained). But this twofold experience does not create an experience of *self*. The self-constitution of the temporal flow is not the constitution of self.

The self-nesting retentions of tones produce a melody, but they do not produce or make present an entity that is hearing it. Zahavi may reply that my insistence on the self-as-entity demands too much: he means the *how* of self-awareness, not the *who*. But a *how* cannot gauge distance from a toy. By the age of 4 months, babies do gauge distance, as shown in the reaching experiments mentioned in Chapter 1. They are aware of themselves as embodied entities and agents. This is the self-awareness I seek to explain.

Husserl made other attempts, appealing to a similarity between the visual comparison of one's body with the body of another. But there are also strong dissimilarities, especially in a baby's experience. He found a bridge, nonetheless, in vocalization. I-the-baby see items, among which are some that emit sounds like the ones I make (carers tend to mimic babies). Without need for conscious reasoning, the animacy that I feel when vocalizing is

---

3 *Der Übergang von Urimpression in Urimpression besagt in Wahrheit, dass die neue mit der unmittelbar retentionalen Wandlung der früheren sich simultan einigt.... Die simultane Einigung ist aber nur möglich als inhaltliche Verschmelzung ....*
4 Take the analogous case of recollection. When I recollect a thing I once perceived, such as a bridge, it appears to memory in the perspective from which I perceived it. But Husserl explicitly rejects the notion that the act of perceiving is recollected (1991, §27).

attributed to those items. Conversely, because I see each of them as a body in the world, I recognize myself to be such a body (Husserl 1989, 101n. with Husserl 1960, §§ 51–54).

Here too we encounter a difficulty. To perceive that an item *vocalizes as I do*, I must be aware that *I* am vocalizing. How shall we account for the embodied self-awareness that is implied by the phrase *vocalizes as I do*? True, the muscular sensations of vocalizing are included in my retentions and protentions, but (to say it again) sensations provide no hint that an entity exists who is sensing them. What does create embodied self-awareness is an event passed over by Husserl: when a carer mimics the sounds that a baby makes, the carer is attending to the baby. From this, we have seen, embodied self-awareness follows at once.

***

The puzzle of self-awareness is this: How can the self, as *object* of awareness, be the *subject* that is aware of it? We have reviewed attempts to answer: proprioception, cerebellar processes, Gibson's ecological insights, the reflection theory, Zahavi's minimal self, and Husserl's studies of time-consciousness. Gibson solves the puzzle, but his most cogent solution does not apply to pre-crawling humans, who are already self-aware. Zahavi solves it, but his theory of the minimal self does not explain the robust self-awareness that we have quite early. What remains is the You-I account.

11

Free will and the You-I account

Arguments against free will often start from the conviction that everything can be reduced to material reality, in which one thing is determined by another that precedes it. In the chain of causality, there is no break, goes the claim, to "shoehorn" freedom in. A practical upshot is that people ought not to be held responsible for their actions, although we may need to quarantine some to protect the rest.

In response, free-will advocates may appeal to chaos theory, emergent complexity, or quantum randomness. But none of these corresponds to the kind of freedom that we feel we have when we decide on an action and carry it out.[1]

We cannot live without making decisions as if free to do so. John Searle writes:

> Imagine that you are in a restaurant and you are given a choice between veal and pork, and you have to make up your mind. You cannot refuse to exercise free will in such a case, because the refusal itself is only intelligible to you as a refusal if you take it as an exercise of free will.
>
> (Searle 2007, 43)

Physical events proceed in a causal chain. One ball strikes another at a certain angle with a certain force, causing it to move in a predictable direction. But when I stand in the voting booth, having reasons to choose a particular candidate, I do not feel forced by the reasons to pull the lever beside her name.

1 On the ways in which these theories fall short, see Sapolsky (2023, Chapters 5–10).

DOI: 10.4324/9781003543275-14

The logical form of ordinary causal explanations is simply that event A caused event B. .... But the form of the explanation of human behavior, where we say that a certain person performed act A by acting on reason R, has a different logical structure .... The form of the explanation is not to give causally sufficient conditions, but to cite the reason that the agent acted on .... It seems that rational action explanations require us to postulate the existence of *an irreducible self*, a rational agent, in addition to the sequence of events.

(Searle 2007, 53; emphasis added)

Where human action is concerned, there is a *gap* in the chain of causality (Searle 2007, 42–43). Because of this gap, in the voting booth I do not feel forced. Likewise, the teacher's question, combined with my knowledge and vanity, may influence me to raise my arm to answer, but what it is like to raise my arm differs fundamentally from what it is like to have it raised by a prankish neighbor. In the latter case, the ascent of the arm is due to a force exerted from outside; it is part of a gapless causal chain. In the former case, the teacher's question, my knowledge, and my vanity do not together force my arm to rise, rather *I* raise it.

As in the example at the restaurant, the experience of free will (not just belief in it) seems to be an indispensable part of our total experience. Much depends, then, on the status we attribute to experience. Should it count as reality? Not in the case of illusions, but there are fundamental experiences without which we could not raise our arms, order a meal, or vote. One of them is the experience of being a self.

So if you say, "Waiter, I'm a determinist—I'll just take whatever comes," where does the *I* come from? We have dealt with the puzzle of self-awareness throughout this book. The solution that works best for humans is the You-I account: the *attentions* of persons—real, mock, or spectral—make and keep me aware of myself. But if we profess to be physical determinists, restricting reality to matter, where do we find an act of attention? To be sure, neurons are material, and attending has neural correlates in the brain of the attender. What is required for self-awareness, however, is an event between brains. Suppose we do brain scans of carer and infant during mutual gaze: In the carer's brain we expect to see neural activity that correlates with an act of attending. In the baby's brain we expect to see a subsequent onset of neural activity, which correlates with the experience of being attended to. We may determine that photons exist between the two sets of eyes, but a photon, as far as we know, does not contain attention. We hear the carer speaking in parentese, we hear the baby's response, and we note the successive vibrations in the air. These do not contain attention either. The determinist may answer that "attentons" will be discovered someday, but the answer merely demonstrates an unscientific *faith* in science.

On first becoming aware of myself, I begin to discover my body (e.g., the feelings at the receiving end of a gaze or the toes in "This little piggy …"). At the core of selfhood, however, is the nonmaterial experience of being attended to. You may claim that our ability to discern another's attention is a product of natural selection among random mutations in living things which emerged from matter, but this claim, if true, would not transform attention into something material. In sum, if the physical determinist could live by what she preaches, poof!—no determinist.

Since our fundamental experiences of other and self cannot be reduced to matter as we know it, does the same hold for our experience of free will? Let us start with a familiar scene from a year or so after infancy.

At the age of 3 years, I-the-child am sitting on your lap facing you. You sing a song. Let the example be one including "Hands on the head …." Singing these words, you put your hands on your head. Then you continue, shifting your hands to your shoulders, nose, mouth, and ears according to the lyrics. You repeat the song with me on your lap day by day, and after a while I perform the same motions in sync with you, singing along. One day, at the point where "on the head" should occur, you sing "on the—" and leave a blank, waiting, your hands frozen halfway up. I may pause like you or continue on my own. The conditions are in place for either: I can stop, since I have merely been shadowing you and you have stopped; but I am also able to continue, because to do so requires nothing more from me than to complete a familiar action that is underway. By pausing, you give me a chance to switch from passive follower to initiator. You place me at a fork in a situation where I have no choice but to choose. In practice, of course, your pause cannot last long: you need to keep the song going. If I do not fill the blank, you do so yourself and continue. But then you create a new blank for "shoulders," and so on. On one of these occasions, I fill the blank—and you respond with delight. Spurred by your approval, I fill the next blank, willing the act. Thus, you solicit my response. You evoke an act of will.

The above is an example, writ large, of something that is always recurring in the back-and-forth of conversation: we pause for each other. It also goes on in carer-infant protoconversation. At this earlier age, however—before self-talk—I-the-baby require your attending for self-awareness. If you pause amid our play, your waiting is a summons. You have opened a blank. I seize the initiative, and my act brings you back into action. I learn that I can have "an impact on parental behavior" (Papoušek 1995, 72). But you did not compel me to seize the initiative. You left it up to me. In choosing to initiate an action or not, I experience free will.

Once this has happened, the experience of free will can extend to situations where reciprocity is not obvious—as when you are absent and I turn to make effects on things that are associated with you. The things lie before me, awaiting my action.

By pausing during interaction with me, you create the causal gap of which Searle writes: an interval in which I can choose how to act, or whether to act at all. What I do amounts to a choice not compelled by you. Many factors will have contributed to the choice I make (e.g., epochs of drought during human evolution), but the immediate factor is you—and *you have suspended yourself as a factor*. This is a crucial point if we recall that, at this early age, you make me aware of myself. By pausing and waiting, you make me aware of myself as free.

Required by you to choose, I probably want to do something you will like, for I am genetically primed to endear you (Chapter 2). But if trust has developed—in particular, if I trust that you will not spurn me for what I choose to do or not—then the choice of action is up to me.

Recall that for no physiological reason, the human baby *pauses* when sucking at the breast or bottle; the pause is met by a jiggle, and at around 2 months, if the jiggle does not come when expected, the baby coos. From the beginning, freedom is built into the relationship. No wonder, then, that the experience of freedom seems fundamental when we order veal.

After the establishment of self-talk, counterfeit You-I Events occur in the mental interior—but here we replicate conversation, the mock others pausing for my response or I for "theirs." The pauses are merely token, since it is I who am playing all parts, and the freedom is token too, but it is never the lockstep of "A causes B." We have seen, furthermore, that work may provide a kind of self-awareness, relieving us from self-talk (Chapter 5). Love may do this too, as may art, conversation, or prayer (Chapters 6, 8, 9, and, we will see, 13). In all these cases, life is interaction with a You—true, mock, or spectral—who pauses for my response.

The experience of freedom originates between persons, not within the nervous system of one.

Determinism

In *Determined*, Robert Sapolsky knows better than to stick with purely physical determinism. He stresses the importance of interaction between the organism and its environment—for example, the effect of early maternal care on the development of the blinking reflex. He errs, however, when he treats the totality of *influences* at any moment as sufficient *cause*. For example, referring to a remark by Donald Trump, Sapolsky writes:

> The question now becomes how readily you come to associate Mexicans with rapists while undergoing Trumpian conditioning—how resistant or vulnerable are you to forming that automatic stereotype in your mind? As usual, it depends on what happened one second before hearing his [Trump's] statement, one minute before, and so on …. Because there are millions of neurons involved, with gazillions of synapses, the process is subject to a lifetime of influences that are staggeringly more complex and nuanced than what goes into conditioning an eyeblink or changing how an Aplysia [a big sea slug] protects its gill. But it's all the same mechanistic building blocks that *will determine* whether your views will be changed by some demagogue's toxic attempt to form a conditioned association in you.
>
> (Sapolsky 2023, 289–90; emphasis added)

Why "will determine"? It often seems that Sapolsky is opposing a straw-man, as if free will requires an utter absence of influences. On the contrary, free will depends on a totality of influences, one of which yields the floor momentarily to me. That is what happens between people when one of them pauses for the other to respond. And since we are always in a form of conversation—or better, "since we *are* a conversation"[2]—the awareness of freedom is integral to our being.

Sapolsky's respect for natural science is such that he does not escape its model of billiard-ball determinism. If he were right—if only "mechanistic

2 *Seit ein Gespräch wir sind und hören voneinander* (Hölderlin *Friedensfeier*).

building blocks" were at work—we would never have to struggle between alternatives: when the factors *for* pulling the trigger outweighed those *against*, the organism would simply pull it. There would be no detour through a conscious weighing of alternatives—the nervous system would spare us the trouble. The strongest neural action-potential would energize the finger, *end of story*. Nor would there follow a feeling of guilt. For conscience says, "You could have done otherwise."

***

Against free will comes an attack from a different quarter. Benjamin Libet found that action is preceded by an electrical uptick in the brain, called a *readiness potential*. His subjects indicated, by means of a signal, the instant they felt an inclination to flex the wrist or press a button. The readiness potential preceded the felt inclination by 350 milliseconds. It would seem that my brain decides without me, and I—conscious I—lumber after it like excess baggage (Libet 1985).

On a closer look, however, Libet's finding holds only for actions performed on a whim, when the results are of no importance to the subject. The readiness potential is "strikingly absent" in the case of deliberate decisions in which the consequence matters (Maoz et al. 2019, 1). It has also been suggested that Libet's finding may be an artificial result of his method; the whim to press on an inconsequential button may be prompted by a preceding uptick in random brain noise (Schurger et al. 2021).

Experience and material reality

It is irksome to be offered two realities: material and experiential. We would prefer one account that encompasses both. Neurologist Kevin J. Mitchell (2023) has recently suggested a way of understanding their relation: All beings are composed of material particles, but in certain beings, including you and me, the particles are organized in such a way that there is a degree of systemic integrity. Just as an individual particle has causal power, so does the organization of particles that is me. My freedom does not collide with causal laws; rather, I am myself a causal factor in a world constrained by causal laws.

Mitchell traces the emergence of living organisms "[f]rom the chemistry of rocks and hydrothermal vents" to systems of interacting molecules, interlocked in dynamic patterns that became self-sustaining. The ones that most robustly maintained their own dynamic organization persisted, replicated, evolved. They became enclosed in a membrane—a tiny subworld unto themselves—exchanging matter and energy with their environment while protecting an internal economy and reconfiguring their own metabolism to adapt to changing conditions.

(Mitchell 2023, 19)

Life, he continues, is in constant struggle against the universal tendency to disorder (as stated in the second law of thermodynamics). An organism needs food for energy to counter that tendency—in other words, to stay organized. In the case of very simple unicellular organisms, their chemistry keeps them bound to a source of food until it is gone; then the chemistry detects a new source and they move toward it. Here nothing intervenes between sensing (food or no food) and action (stay or move). In such a case, there is no free will. But with the evolution of multicellular organisms, including neurons that transmitted signals between the cells,

[p]erception and action were decoupled by layers of intervening cells. Instead of being acted on singly and immediately like a reflex, multiple sensory signals could be simultaneously conveyed to central processing regions and operated on in a common space.

(Mitchell 2023, 20)

The complicated, highly organized entity needs to make choices for staying organized. To deliberate among possibilities, it must know it is free to choose one. But how does it know it is free? For humans, the question returns us to the carer and infant in protoconversation. The carer repeatedly makes the infant self-aware, and while doing so she opens causal gaps. In creating me, you create me free.

Where does the You-I theory fit in discussions of free will?

When we moderns wish to explain something, we are guided by the immense explanatory power of the natural sciences, so we seek a determin-istic chain. It goes against our grain to accept a concept of free will unless it is *compatible* with determinism. One approach, found in Spinoza and Nietzsche, is to say that freedom consists in adopting as our own the forces that determine our decisions. If you can't beat determinism, join it. Other compatibilists distinguish between internal factors, such as desires and reasons, and external factors; we have free will, they say, when the external factors do not constrain us, leaving a role for the internal. Then comes the question as to how the internal desires and reasons were formed. What if they were formed by forces beyond one's control—in the deep evolutionary past, for example? If so, may we count the self as free?

In fidelity to the *experience* of free will, we should not reduce the self to its desires and reasons. The self exists as an entity in its own right. Moreover, the experience of a free self seems fundamental, for (recalling the exchange at the restaurant) we could not function without it.

The theory proposed in this chapter admits all the conceivable factors that influence behavior, including, in the baby's case, the enormous factor of the carer. Free will originates during early interaction, when this great factor pauses—puts its influence on hold—leaving an opening into which I-the-baby may act or not.[3] In other words, yes, there is a totality of factors— a completely determined situation—but one of the principal factors withdraws, confronting me with an opening into which I may act. And what shall I do, if anything? There is, indeed, an *arbitrariness* about the choice I will make or not make (for not to choose is a choice). No matter what I do, or even if I do nothing, after a certain time the carer responds and the interaction continues, until she pauses again. She creates my freedom and trains me in it.

In this original experience of freedom, any choice I make might just as easily not be made. The choice may seem ungrounded in reasons or desires—mere play, just part of the fun. This arbitrariness is lost when self-talk restructures experience. Henceforth we live in flight from our absolute dependence on others, under compulsion of self-talk. Can such a life be called free? Our supposedly free choices are derived from the projects we adopted from people we internalized. The projects determine our interests and actions. Now, indeed, we have reasons for what we do. We experience free will when we act, but it is a limited freedom, which we may

---

3 Perhaps needless to say, I am not referring to the still-face experiment, which requires an unnatural distortion of the pauses that are part of every protoconversation.

attribute to the token pauses of self-talk or to the pauses of the diminished others outside. The prisoner is free to move in her cell.

It is largely by means of frames, we have seen, that we get free from the compulsion to talk with ourselves. We find a vestige of our original freedom, for example, in the conversations-for-their-own-sake that were discussed in Chapter 9: insights and humor emerge that no participant knew in advance. These are the products, I said, of a meeting between the split-off selves of the conversers. Recall the pun of the oxymoron, as well as the faux pas. They pop into the space between us without forethought. The space between us is the locale of freedom, first established during the You-I Events of infancy, and although it is well hidden amid the general mistrust of later life, a lively conversation restores it within the bounds of a frame.

In the original experience of freedom, the arbitrariness is like an abyss into which I am called to leap, but the abyss is not entirely or predominantly dreadful. It is ruled by the expectant, affirming smile of the carer, whom I trust to respond.

12

The call of conscience

A special kind of You-I Event

Philosopher Bernhard Waldenfels writes: "The principle of gaining oneself through giving oneself is initially a law of life; it first becomes a moral commandment in the view of the distorted life."[1] Why "initially a law of life"? Because in infancy it functions without my having to learn it. I have no awareness of my existence except through others. Their importance to me is absolute, and so I cannot betray them. True, I permit only certain carers to bestow self-awareness on me. I can snub the babysitter by playing with things that are imbued by an absent carer. Present or absent, nevertheless, there must be a You.

The onset of self-talk radically modifies this condition. Since I no longer need other people to make me aware of myself, no one *appears* to me in the absolute importance that carers once had. The You-I Event ceases to be a law of life, appearing instead as a moral commandment. The latter is expressed in well-known exhortations: "Do unto others as you would have them do unto you." "Love the other as yourself." "Reciprocity."

Even within the domain of self-talk, however, a trace of the original carers survives in the concept of a *person*. A person is an entity that can, in principle, make me aware of myself. After self-talk has been established, everyone I encounter is a *potential but precluded You*.

The call of conscience is often a call from the potential You in a person I have hurt. It need not come in words. More often it occurs as a feeling of guilt, which gives me to understand: "You who did this, something is basically wrong with you, that you would do such a thing." The same

1 *Der Satz vom Selbstgewinn durch Selbsthingabe ist zunächst ein Lebensgesetz; zu einem moralischen Gebot wird es erst in der Sicht des gestörten Lebens* (Waldenfels 1971, 307).

DOI: 10.4324/9781003543275-15

holds for things I should have done but neglected to do and for things that I believe are evil but would like to do. Memories crop up by themselves—of a thoughtless remark, of a letter left unanswered or one I should not have written, of a damaging lie, of a poorly aimed gift, of missing a date, of disregard for someone whose love I took for granted. Or I find myself joking to disabled people about their disability: midway through the punchline, the import of what I am saying arches back and drenches me like a wave. What demon has led me to seek out her weak spot and pick at it? "It is not a demon," says conscience, "It is you!"

Often we get involved in situations of greater ethical complexity than these misdeeds, but the simple examples point to a principle: When I hurt someone and later feel guilt, she appears in a fullness I had failed to see. This is the fullness of a You.

Consider the thoughtless, wounding remark. It is created by the same split-off self that fashions dreams and slips of the tongue. Most likely, I would not have made it to someone who has power over me. I would have "watched my tongue" (rehearsing it with a mock other before saying it). However, when someone is irrelevant to my projects, my guard is down and out it springs.

"I did not mean it," I say, but conscience does not accept a plea of self-division. The split-off self who spoke is me; I brought this hurt into the world. I may plead that I began self-talk so young, so unaware of its consequences, and with such encouragement from carers, that I can hardly be blamed for the split in the self. Conscience is not swayed.

Or suppose that the harm I do is deliberate. If later I feel guilt, I cannot disarm my conscience by pleading that an alien impulse possessed me, or that I was a different person then, or that I was following government orders (the nation can change its policies, but nothing can change the fact that I did what I did). The wounded one, returning in memory, bursts the frame of the philosophy that justified me. In all these cases, whether the act was deliberate or not, the potential You—the You I failed to see—points at me.

The call of conscience is a kind of You-I Event, making me aware of myself, but this self-awareness differs from that of infancy. The difference stems from the fact that self-talk has altered the structure of experience. The call pertains to that altered structure. It makes me present to myself not as a unity, rather in self-division. I am brought to a stop by the You in the wounded one, until something occurs to release me—apology and forgiveness, perhaps—or until I am sufficiently distracted.

More than half a century later, she will perhaps have forgotten, or she may be dead, but her eyes (whether I saw them then or only picture them now) can freeze me in my tracks, reuniting me with the self of that time who did that thing.

Racism preempts the pain of guilt

Paul Bloom makes a case that race matters to a baby "only insofar as it piggybacks on *coalition*" (2013, 64 citing Kurzban et al. 2001). Humans form We-versus-Them coalitions according to any available criterion: language, accent, skin color, shirt color, hometown, school, or a coin toss (Bloom 2013, 69–70). The tendency has an evolutionary background. Chimpanzees live in groups that attack one another, often for no discernible reason. They do not form intergroup alliances (Smith 2011, 213). From the last of the ancestors we shared with them, we inherited our tendency to intergroup hostility. In our case, though, it is offset by another factor, with the consequence that our groups *do* make alliances.

The offsetting factor is the one that has been the theme of this book. As argued in Chapter 2, humans are born predisposed to the You-I Event. During most of our evolution, each human baby had several carers, unlike chimps and the other great apes, who know only one. At 2 years old, we are about equal to chimps of that age in cognitions of space, causality, and quantity, as well as in the use of tools. However, our social-cognitive abilities are greater and keep increasing (Tomasello 2019, 29). Now, recall the claim that the You of the Event constitutes the meaning *person*. When my group encounters members of another group, my chimp-related predisposition to attack is offset by the fact that I recognize them as persons. In other words, something in me knows what I, the secure self, long ago ceased to know: that any of them could, in principle, make me aware of myself.

The distinctive pain of guilt is felt when I violate a relationship. I could not deliberately violate it when I depended on the other for self-awareness. After mastering self-talk, though, I *can* do so while remaining self-aware. Yet the You *bites back*, as reflected in the English speaker's *re-morse*, the Italian's *rimorso di coscienza*, and the German's *Gewissensbisse*. The prototype may have been the first great lesson in socialization: recall that breastfed babies must learn not to bite at the nipple, for biting (unintentionally) breaks the relationship.

It is possible, however, to harm other people while avoiding the pain of guilt. The carers who made me self-aware were human; guilt is felt especially in relation to humans. To avoid the pain when my group oppresses another group, the logical move is to negate or diminish the other group's humanity.

For example, as a White boy in a White suburb of New York City in the 1950s, I was troubled by the lower status of those we called "colored." I idolized Jackie Robinson, but the only Black people I saw in person were servants. A child wants an explanation (though I never asked): "Why do they clean up after us? What makes this OK?" I did not want to think that my parents shared in oppression. I was tempted to accept, therefore, a notion which seemed evident in the behavior of fellow Whites: that people of color do not count as persons to the same degree. This did not need utterance.

We benefited from their services. No house lacked a "maid." They came by bus every morning from Jamaica, NY and were gone by evening. I saw them as if through a scrim. Everyone on our side was clearly visible, but everyone on their side was dimmer. Their humanity was dimmer. It would be unfitting to feel guilt. If they were like us, why didn't they revolt? Wouldn't *we*? How could they be counted on not to? What kept us safe? It must be that everyone involved, even they, was of the same view concerning their place in the hierarchy of being. This ranking proceeded quite outside awareness. Researchers have studied White Americans who declare themselves to be free of racial prejudice. In tests using word-pairs and demanding quick answers, it was found that most unwittingly associated Blacks with negative concepts and their fellow Whites with positive (J. M. Jones et al. 2013, 188–89).

It is easier to diminish the potential You in the members of another group when they are distinct in color or language or customs. According to one suggestion, our inherited ability to distinguish biological species evolved, by a process called *exaptation*, into a predisposition to distinguish between human groups as if they were separate species (Gil-White 2001). From here it is a short step to believing that one's own group is the only fully human one. Dehumanization "appears in the East and in the West, among sophisticates of the developed world and among remote Amazonian tribes" (Smith 2011, 25). Its success depends on the need to belong. The implicit message: If you're one of us, you'll call them *gooks* (a term applied to Viet Cong guerrillas). And why do I need to belong? Because I still depend absolutely on others, namely people I have internalized. I join my group in negating the potential You in members of another. I firebomb "krauts," "japs," "gooks."

Despite a group's efforts to dehumanize rival groups, the You in them cannot be expunged. Regarding Post-Traumatic Stress Disorder (PTSD), researchers have discovered "the profound impact that taking another life in the context of combat may have on veterans .... Killing was associated with PTSD symptoms, peritraumatic dissociation, functional impairment, and violent behaviors, after controlling for exposure to general combat" (Maguen et al. 2009, 441, 443). The rate of suicide among war veterans is much higher than that of same-age nonveterans. In a 1991 study of 100 combat veterans from the Vietnam War, 19 had tried to kill themselves at least once since the war, and another 15 had been preoccupied with the idea. The researchers found that "the presence of persistent guilt related to wartime experiences provided the sharpest contrast between the suicide attempters and the non-suicidal veterans." Depression "plays a role which is clearly secondary to that of guilt about combat actions" (Hendin and Haas, 1991, 588–90). Dehumanization had not done the trick. The You in the "gook" had not been expunged.

The You cannot be expunged. This fact, together with certain other facts we can all observe, suggests a kind of spiral. When we dehumanize a group, the potential You in each of its members does not disappear. It sneaks around back. Judging *them* to be less than human, we believe they are lacking in the restraints imposed by civilization (i.e., by our mock others). When we attribute to them this freedom from inhibition, they appear to possess an animal vitality, but they retain a measure of intelligence (e.g., they can speak, although "badly" by our standards). Animal vitality plus intelligence form a dangerous combination. The result is a category between human and beast: the *demon*. Fearing such a creature, we oppress it to keep it down. But the You cannot be expunged. Consequently, the more we keep the demon down, the more guilt we will feel unless we dehumanize further. The more we dehumanize, the more demonic they seem. The more demonic they seem, the deeper our dread of them. The deeper our dread of them, the harder we push them down. The harder we push them down, the more guilt we will feel unless we dehumanize further, and so on.

The spiral begins, as said, when we take measures to preempt the bite of guilt, which can be traced to the You-I Event. By the trick of dehumanization, the epitome of good is twisted into evil. No doubt there is an evolutionary component (recall the chimps), but—to echo Nietzsche—the human beast is cruelest. Our extra measure of cruelty comes from the exceptional contribution of the You-I Event to making us who we are.

The spiral of evil can begin from anything that causes one coalition to dehumanize another. In the case of my White suburb, the only way to break it would have been to establish equal opportunities. A child should not have to seek explanations for oppression. The spiral will not cease until there is no oppression to explain.[2]

Huck and Jim on the raft

Sometimes, against the odds, a member of the dehumanized group appears to the dehumanizers on an equal footing with them. In such a case, conscience may call, unseating the mock others who usually co-opt it. The best-known literary example is *Huckleberry Finn* (Twain 1885).[3] Huck, a White boy of 14, is escaping from his abusive father as well as from Miss Watson, who has been trying to "civilize" him. Jim, a Black adult, is also escaping from Miss Watson, who owns him. Starting in Missouri, a slave-state, they float down the Mississippi on a raft; Jim is aiming for Cairo, Illinois, where he can be free. A friendship develops. At one point (in Chapter XV), thick fog sets in. Huck paddles out ahead in his canoe to seek a place to tie the raft until the fog lifts, but the raft is soon enshrouded. The current bears him along, and after a night of hollering for Jim he gives up and falls asleep. The next morning, he spots the raft and catches up to it. Jim is asleep at the oar. Huck wakes him, pretending that he'd been there all night and that Jim had dreamed up the fog. Jim falls for this, and then Huck, laughing, reveals the truth. Jim responds to his mirth by describing how his heart was almost broken when he thought Huck was lost, how he had given up caring what would happen to himself, how he had fallen asleep at the oar, and what a relief it had been to see Huck safe and sound, how tears had come, and how he could have gotten down on his knees and kissed Huck's foot, he was so thankful—but all Huck had been thinking was how to make a fool of him.

That was enough, reports Huck. "It made me feel so mean I could almost kissed *his* foot to get him to take it back."

They are not at Miss Watson's now, nor on the land that belongs to the White coalition. Jim is free on the raft. He speaks like an equal, saying what

2 I first analyzed the spiral of evil in Langfur (2023/1992).
3 Some find racism in this book. I view it as an antidote to racism, in agreement with Wayne C. Booth (1998).

he feels. Huck's self-awareness, for a change, does not come from a mock
Miss Watson or a mock Judge Thatcher or his mock "pappy." It comes from
Jim, whom he has hurt.

The next night they resume their journey, looking for the lights of Cairo.
It occurs to Huck that Jim is almost free— "and who was to blame for it?
Why, *me*. I couldn't get that out of my conscience, no how nor no way." To
whom belongs the voice of conscience in this sentence? To a mock You: the
White coalition.

But Cairo had eluded them in the fog. The river carries them into the
slave states of the South. They get separated again. In Chapter XXXI, Huck
learns that Jim has been caught, although the captors do not know who
owns him. Huck pens a letter to Miss Watson, giving her Jim's location. On
lifting his eyes from the paper …

> I felt good and all washed clean of sin for the first time I had ever felt
> so in my life, and I knowed I could pray now. But I didn't do it straight
> off, but laid the paper down and set there thinking—thinking how good
> it was all this happened so, and how near I come to being lost and going
> to hell. And went on thinking. And got to thinking over our trip down
> the river; and I see Jim before me all the time: in the day and in the
> night-time, sometimes moonlight, sometimes storms, and we a-floating
> along, talking and singing and laughing. But somehow I couldn't seem
> to strike no places to harden me against him, but only the other kind.
> I'd see him standing my watch on top of his'n, 'stead of calling me, so
> I could go on sleeping; and see him how glad he was when I come back
> out of the fog … and then I happened to look around and see that paper.
>
> It was a close place. I took it up, and held it in my hand. I was
> a-trembling, because I'd got to decide, forever, betwixt two things, and
> I knowed it. I studied a minute, sort of holding my breath, and then says
> to myself: "All right, then, I'll go to hell"—and tore it up.

Huck's dilemma is not between two equally valid calls of conscience. It is
between the call of a mock You and the call of a You. But a relativist might
argue: "Isn't the call of Miss Watson—that Huck should help her get her
property back— also the call of a You? Why should the Watson-You count
less than the Jim-You? It's just a matter of viewpoint, and there's no criterion
by which to judge between them." But there is a criterion! A You is an entity
that can make me self-aware. A You cannot be owned, controlled, or possessed, because the You-I Event requires another person, and the moment

I believe I control you, I have lost sight of your otherness. The fact that a You cannot be owned puts Miss Watson and her coalition in the wrong.

A You can be in the wrong. A You may bring me to presence by an act of attending even when the attention is hostile, narrow-minded, bigoted, indifferent, or sadistic. The resulting self-awareness may be brittle or negative (recall the negative You-I Event), but I am nonetheless present to myself through the You. I can struggle with a You, as babies sometimes struggle with their carers, and I can also punish a You. But to the extent that I see a person as the You that she in principle is, there are things I cannot do: I cannot kill her, because this would amount to killing an entity that can create me as a self. I cannot own her, because this would be to lose sight of the otherness that is essential to a You. I cannot envy her, disrespect her, betray her, or rob her (unless robbing her means liberating a potential You, as in the case of Jim). Each of these acts would harm one who can be, in principle, the source of my existence as a self.

What kind of argument, then, can we raise against someone who claims, "What's right in Miss Watson's eyes is right for her, what's right in my eyes is right for me, and there's no way of deciding"? Here is an argument, in support of which empirical findings were presented in Part 1. It moves from what *is* the case in infancy to how I *should* behave:

1 Given the evolution of animal life, we are typically born with a preference for existence rather than death.
2 Awareness of my existence requires the You-I Event.
3 Therefore, each You is absolutely important to me.
4 An entity is a potential You if it can, in principle, make me aware of my being. Such an entity is called a *person*.
5 After self-talk has been established, each person I encounter is both a diminished other and a potential but precluded You.

(Now we shift from *is* to *should*.)

6 Each diminished other should *count* for me as a You, because it is I who am responsible for the self-talk which prevents her from appearing as a You.
7 Conclusion: I should treat each person as absolutely important.

"So act," wrote Kant, "as to treat humanity, whether in your own person or in that of any other, in every case at the same time as an end, never as a means only" (Kant 2005, 88). This maxim is grounded in the You-I Event.

Counterfeit morality

When I play others toward myself, I include their attitudes, which may then get conflated with the voice of conscience, co-opting its power. The moral law originates in the You-I Event, but some so-called morals are decreed by mock others.

We find this mixture in Jonathan Haidt's *The Righteous Mind* (2012). In Chapters 7 and 8, he picks out six "foundations of morality": (1) care vs. harm, (2) fairness vs. cheating, (3) liberty vs. oppression, (4) loyalty to the group vs. betrayal, (5) authority vs. subversion, and (6) sanctity vs. degradation. The first three foundations are rooted in the You-I Event: (1) I care for someone on whom my sense of my existence could, in principle, depend; (2) I treat her fairly; and (3) the Event cannot occur unless she is other, hence free.

After self-talk is established, the Event ceases to be a law of life, becoming a source of moral commandments. The commandments will vary, depending on the values affirmed by mock others. When they represent one group against other groups, the first three foundations are twisted: (1a) Care only for your own kind (e.g., Huck's White coalition); (2a) be fair to them, but it's OK to cheat outsiders; and (3a) don't let anyone oppress your group, but it's all right to oppress non-members.

Now consider the last three of Haidt's "foundations of morality": (4) loyalty to the coalition vs. betrayal, (5) authority vs. subversion, and (6) sanctity vs. degradation. None is inherent in the You-I Event, although each, like it, has an evolutionary background.

The fourth foundation (loyalty) arises in a situation of embattled coalitions. It may be part of our genetic inheritance: in coalitions where loyalty prevailed, the members were more likely to survive and reproduce, transmitting the trait of loyalty to new generations.

As for the fifth foundation (authority vs. subversion), when group size grew beyond the ties of kinship, respect for hierarchical authority held the group together. The You-I Event, by contrast, is marked by equality as well as authority: bestowing self-awareness, the You seems powerful indeed, but I become present to myself as a being that is fundamentally like her, hence equal in importance.

The sixth and last of Haidt's moral foundations is sanctity vs. degradation. He thinks that religion is a byproduct of our highly adaptive tendency to detect agency in events.

[S]uppose that early humans ... begin to talk about their many misper-
ceptions. Suppose they begin attributing agency to the weather. (Thunder and lightning sure make it seem as though somebody up in the sky
is angry at us.) .... Voilà—the birth of supernatural agents, not as an
adaptation for anything but as a by-product of a cognitive module that is
otherwise highly adaptive.

(Haidt 2012, 292)

This byproduct, he points out, must have been vital in the competition
between groups. Those who pray together stay together. Furthermore, if
you believe that your group's god is watching, you are less likely to break
the rules (reportedly commanded by that god). For example, you are less
likely to take a free ride on other members' labor. In this way, religion
shapes a more cohesive and enduring society. Haidt gives the example of
200 communes in the 19th-century USA: "[J]ust 6 percent of the secular
communes were still functioning twenty years after their founding, compared to 39 percent of the religious communes" (p. 297). In short, faith
pays. We have inherited the genes of believers.

I will be discussing faith in the next chapter. I think there is more to it
than thunder and lightning. For now, though, let us continue with Haidt's
foundations. As said, the last three of the six—loyalty, authority, and
sanctity—do not derive directly from the You-I Event. They have nothing to do with what I have called the main moral commandment, but they
do contribute powerfully to group cohesion. Haidt calls them "the binding
foundations" (p. 316). When groups compete for survival, these foundations are vital. Yet they are not *moral*. For why should Group A survive
rather than B? No answer—except that A is my group.

Morality binds and blinds, says Haidt (p. 218). He means that it holds
my group together while blinding us to the humanity of non-members. In a
democracy, he notes, conservatives have a gene-based electoral advantage,
because liberals appeal to only three of the six foundations (care, fairness,
and liberty), neglecting the rest, whereas conservatives appeal to all six. The
implication is that if society were left to the liberals, it would fall apart. This
is the fear to which conservatives are more sensitive, and Haidt advises that
liberals listen to them. At stake is "the miracle of moral communities that
grow beyond the bounds of kinship" (p. 339). "The process of converting
pluribus (diverse people) into *unum* (a nation) is a miracle that occurs in

every successful nation on Earth. Nations decline or divide when they stop performing this miracle" (p. 193).

The point is a good one, but we ought not to conflate morality with what binds and blinds. According to Haidt's six foundations, what should Huck have done? The balance comes out heavily on the side of sending the letter to Miss Watson. By tearing it up, he fails to care for her, is not fair to her, weakens his coalition's freedom to own slaves, is disloyal to it, refuses to respect its authority, and acts in defiance of its God. Yet tearing it up is the morally right thing to do—and not blind. So morality must reside elsewhere than in Haidt's foundations.

Haidt is aware of the problem (p. 316). He defines morality as a system of values, virtues, norms, practices, and other factors "that work together to suppress or regulate self-interest and make cooperative societies possible." This definition, he admits, cannot stand alone. It is merely descriptive, not *normative*: A normative definition would "specify what is really and truly right, regardless of what anyone thinks" (pp. 314–15). If his definition were proposed as normative, "it would give high marks to fascist and communist societies" (p. 316). Instead, he proposes that we take it as an adjunct to normative theories. Of the latter, however, he writes very little, allotting top slot to the utilitarian idea of the greatest good for the greatest number. He does not say what the good would be. And no wonder! After all, who can say what the good is?

We can. The good is the You-I Event. More exactly, the Event is as good as existence is good, since the Event is what makes me aware that I exist. True, you may rightly ask me to justify the assertion that existence is good. The best I can do is to rehearse the evolutionary argument of Chapter 2. We take existence to be good because we possess the genes of just those animals that found it good: the ones that willed to go on living long enough to reproduce.

In line with Haidt's first three foundations, the moral commandment is to behave toward each person as a You, since it is I the self-talker who preclude her appearing thus. The commandment does not help in situations where we must choose between saving one potential You or another. What we *should* do, however, is work toward a social order in which we will never have to face such dilemmas, at least not because of circumstances created or allowed by us.

13

God or the precluded You

This chapter lies under the burden of a principle enunciated by Irving Greenberg. Speaking of the children who were thrown into the fiery pit at Auschwitz, he writes: "No statement, theological or otherwise, should be made that would not be credible in the presence of the burning children" (1977, 23; on the children, p. 9).

In view of the sufferings that people and other animals sometimes undergo, how can anyone believe in a being who is all-powerful, all-knowing, and morally perfect? There are various approaches to this question. Not all of them measure up to Greenberg's principle.

***

From the thought of John Calvin, philosopher Alvin Plantinga adopts the notion of a *sensus divinitatis*, claiming that in addition to our other senses (sight, smell, etc.), we possess a faculty for sensing God. He holds that its seed exists from birth, but as life goes on, sin distorts it. If the *sensus divinitatis* were to develop in a person without distortion, she would know God as surely as she knows anything. Such a person "would have an intimate, detailed, vivid, and explicit knowledge of God; she would have an intense awareness of his presence, glory, goodness, [and] power …; and she would be as convinced of God's existence as of her own" (Plantinga 2015, 202).

Plantinga adds that this person's conviction would not be shaken by the occurrence of evil. She might, however, be perplexed. She …

> might ask herself why God permits it …. If she finds no answer, she will no doubt conclude that God has a reason that is beyond her ken; she won't be in the least inclined to doubt that there *is* such a person as God.
> (Plantinga 2015, 202)

DOI: 10.4324/9781003543275-16

Plantinga is arguing for God's reality, which, if we did not sin, we would be as equipped to know as well as we know anything. Yet something falls short in the comparison. If a trusted friend permits evils that he could have prevented, we ask him why; if he does not answer and continues to permit them, we do not stop at perplexity. Our trust in him wanes. Should it not be the same with God? In the face of the sufferings that go unexplained, shouldn't we either doubt his power to prevent them or doubt his goodness—or doubt the *sensus divinitatis*?

In this chapter I will doubt the *sensus divinitatis*. I hold instead that we enter the world with a *sensus humanitatis*, namely, a genetically primed readiness to encounter a You. Birth is followed by a period of You-I Events. Beginning in the 3rd year, our self-talk precludes them, for reasons we have seen. Like sin in the Calvin-Plantinga scheme, self-talk distorts the structure of experience, leaving us with an unconscious yearning for the You we preclude. This yearning may come to expression as a yearning for God.

The problem of evil

Rather than doubt the *sensus divinitatis*, Plantinga has offered the following solution to the problem of evil. God's omnipotence cannot override logical necessity. He could not *both* make us free *and* keep us from doing evil. He chose our freedom as the greater good, forgoing control over us. If God were to limit our freedom to such an extent that we could not do evil, it would hardly be a freedom worth having.

The difficulty with this solution is that it makes God hardly worth worshiping. If he set things going and departed forever, would the sheer fact of his existence render our lives more meaningful? Would it help us if we managed to discover that he observes from afar, rejoicing and weeping with us, but is resolved to keep hands off? If the most he can do is commiserate, humans can do that too.

At one point in a powerful book about suffering (more powerful in putting the question than answering it), Harold Kushner accepts the idea that for the sake of our free will, God keeps hands off. But that does not make him irrelevant, Kushner claims. "How does God make a difference in our lives if He neither kills nor cures? God inspires people to help other people who have been hurt by life ...." (1981, 139).

This answer falls short. Huck Finn did not need God's inspiration when it came to freeing Jim. On the contrary, he believed that God would be sending him to hell for doing so. But we need not resort to fiction. We can all think of atrocities that have drawn inspiration from a putatively omnipotent, omniscient, morally perfect God.

The Bible maintains human freedom while portraying a God who intervenes. Although he seems unavailable much of the time, he is not above hearing the cries of Hebrew slaves and returning to divide the sea. The contradiction between a freedom worth having and a God worth worshipping is biblically resolved by *miracles*.

There is no reason why divine miracles and human freedom cannot coexist, as in the Bible. What is more, in the promised Kingdom of Heaven, will not God be actively present and his worshippers free? If he can coexist with free humans in the future, why not here and now?

Still further: In our earthly life, God could combine our freedom with his interventions by keeping miracles rare.[1] Noting the rarity, humans would still be correct in feeling free. He could also keep the miracles secret. (You may answer that secret miracles might be happening now and always, but we have seen enough evil to tip the scale against this idea.) In sum, if God could have secretly prevented, by a stitch in time, the millions of horrible and pointless sufferings that humans have known, how can we think of him as good?

Paranormal events do happen: a jar explodes by itself at the very moment when a religious fast should start; a poster featuring your mother's first name leads you to phone her in the nick of time; a psychic directs you to a lost wedding ring. There are more things in heaven and earth than are dreamt of in our philosophies. But when it is a question of an intervening God, the horrors decide the matter.

Nor can the problem of evil be avoided by saying "God's ways are mysterious." True, human cognition is limited. But what can his moral perfection mean to us if it does not connect with morality as we understand it? Here I agree with Harold Kushner: "A parent who disciplines a child for doing something wrong, but never tells him what he is being punished for, is hardly a model of responsible parenthood" (1981, 23).

Like the Sinner Man of the song, the believer runs from shelter to shelter—from theodicy to theodicy—until he arrives at the Devil. In the spirit of the Apostle Paul, who wrote of "powers" and "principalities," C. S. Lewis (2001) proposes that when God withdrew for the sake of our

1 This paragraph draws from Tooley (2021).

freedom, the Devil took over. Plantinga also raises the idea (1989, 58). David Bentley Hart appeals to it in *The Doors of the Sea*. He describes the Indian Ocean tsunami of 2004, which killed more than 150,000 people. It was not God's doing, he writes.

> [W]e exist in the long melancholy aftermath of a primordial catastrophe .... [T]he universe languishes in bondage to the "powers" and "principalities" of this age .... To say that God elects to fashion rational creatures in his image, and so grants them the freedom to bind themselves and the greater physical order to *another master*—to say that he who sealed up the doors of the sea might permit them to be opened again by *another, more reckless hand*—is not to say that God's ultimate design for his creatures can be thwarted.
>
> (Hart 2005, 58; emphases added)

So, God's departure from the world is not forever. His self-restraint and the Devil's rule are temporary. In fact, writes Lewis, followed by Hart, God's return is already happening. Two thousand years ago, he sent his only son to foment a revolt against the "other master." The revolt is Christianity—not all that goes by the name, but a way of being in which the believer is able to look beyond the horrors, discern a love that is "not of this world" (John 18:36), and bind herself to it. Sometime in the future, after we have had many chances to freely join the revolt, God will cut bait, defeat the Devil, and lead us into his Kingdom.

Against the intellectual fashions of their days, Lewis and Hart readmit the Devil; this willingness to buck the Enlightenment shows that they recognize how extremely difficult the problem is. Apart from the weirdness, however (the Devil caused the tsunami?), the appeal to God's future Kingdom is flawed by disregard for the nature of time. "Thy Kingdom come," the Christian prays, as does the Jew in the Kaddish. Suppose it come. Not all evils suffered in time can be compensated in eternity. Holocaust scholar Alice Eckardt writes:

> We need to keep in mind the particularly obscene forms of suffering and helplessness the Nazi "Final Solution" imposed on its special victims: .... In the ghetto stage it encompassed the torturous choice a father or mother sometimes had to make as to which child to give over to a rescuer, or which parent or spouse should receive the precious work permit or hiding place.
>
> (Eckardt 1994, 11 n. ii)

For a parent, the fact of having chosen which child to rescue and which not to rescue cannot be undone in God's Kingdom. After we have entered its glory, we may locate the parent and tell her, "For the sake of human freedom, the powers of evil could not be stopped from ruling the world in which you were forced to choose. But now those powers are vanquished, and here we are, and here are your resurrected children, living in eternal joy with God." The joy of the parent cannot be complete, nor can that of the children. The choice that was made cannot be erased. Lived time is irrevocable.

Mind or matter—or?

Several arguments for God begin from an either/or: either we believe that the mind cannot be reduced to matter (and the writer then traces the mind to its source in God), or we believe that matter is all.

Materialism (aka physicalism, naturalism) is the idea that reality amounts to nothing but bits of matter interacting. Against this idea stands the fact that it *is* an idea. An idea means something, and you cannot get meanings from matter alone—more exactly, not from matter as we currently know it. The materials in a brick do not carry the meaning *brick*, not even when arranged and baked as one. To a person from a nonbuilding culture, the product of the baking would not mean *brick*. The meaning derives from a cultural practice. It is practiced by selves. According to this book, each self is the product of another self's attending. As said in Chapter 11, matter does not suffice to constitute an act of attending or the experience of being attended to: there are photons but not attentons.

Because meanings exist, matter as we know it cannot be all. But does this leave God as the sole explanation for meaning? We will discuss three phenomena which believers have used in arguing for God: conscience, desire, and reason. Behind the *sensus divinitatis* we will find, in each case, the *sensus humanitatis*.

The argument from conscience

C. S. Lewis writes of his conversion from atheism to faith: "My argument against God was that the universe seemed so cruel and unjust. But how had I got this idea of *just* and *unjust?*" (2001, 31–32).

We saw how in the previous chapter (12). In my beginning, a You is indispensable to me, because it is through a You that I am aware of my existence. After self-talk is established, each person I encounter is both a diminished other and a potential but precluded You. Each diminished other should *count* for me as a You, because it is I who am responsible for the self-talk which prevents her from appearing as such. Therefore, I should treat each person as absolutely important. To do otherwise is to act unjustly.

The full meaning of *person* is reasserted in the call of conscience. It is not God who calls. It is the person I should have seen—that is, the You I could have seen, if I did not exist in a world restructured by my own self-talk.

The argument from desire

> The Christian says, 'Creatures are not born with desires unless satisfaction for those desires exists …. If I find in myself a desire which no experience *in this world* can satisfy, the most probable explanation is that I was made for another world.'
>
> (Lewis 2001, 113; emphasis added)

In place of "this world," read "the world as it appears when restructured by self-talk." In place of "another world," read "the world constituted by the joint-attentional You-I Event." After self-talk has become habitual, the yearning for a You persists outside awareness. The yearning is the "desire which no experience in this world can satisfy"; that is, the yearning cannot be filled by diminished others and diminished things.[2]

Lewis writes that a person

> must come at last to the clear knowledge that the human soul was made to enjoy some *object that is never fully given* – nay, cannot even be imagined as given – in our present mode of subjective and spatio-temporal experience. This Desire was, in the soul, as the Siege Perilous in Arthur's castle—the chair in which only one could sit. And if nature makes nothing in vain, the One who can sit in this chair must exist.
>
> (Lewis 1977, 15; emphasis added)

---

2 Cf. Mills (2016, 91–92). Mills proposes that the term *God* "represents … a particular psychic reality, the semiotic voice of an inner calling" and ponders whether this calling may be "a human emotive expression primarily based in lack."

To the contrary! I hold that the "object" of our unfulfilled yearning *was* fully given. True, the You of that time "cannot even be imagined as given—in our present mode of subjective and spatio-temporal experience." But this is our mode of experience after self-talk has restructured it.

The difference between C. S. Lewis' position and mine is this: he takes the desire that cannot be fulfilled in "this world" as desire for God; I take it as desire for a You who is dreaded, precluded, and forgotten. His position is challenged by the evidence of horrible, pointless suffering. In contrast, there is no evidence against the yearning for a You. Admittedly, we have neither access to such a being nor memory of it, and the yearning is unconscious. We have seen why this is so, and considerations have been given for an early structure in which the You was present.

The argument from reason

The Reason that exists in each of us must have come from somewhere. Whether you trace it to genetic inheritance or culture or a combination of both,

> [s]ooner or later you must admit a Reason which exists absolutely on its own. The problem is whether you or I can be such a self-existent Reason .... Now it is clear that my reason has grown up gradually since my birth and is interrupted for several hours each night. I therefore cannot be that eternal self-existent Reason .... [Each human mind] has its tap-root in an eternal, self-existent, rational Being, whom we call God.
>
> (Lewis 1967, 32)

True, we do not know where Reason comes from, but at least one other explanation is conceivable: A chaotic universe could not have produced so complex and stable a phenomenon as life, much less brains that reason. There may have been many chaotic universes, but eventually a universe formed that was regular enough for living things to emerge—that is, things whose cells could grow and split into daughter cells (Cox and Cohen 2015, 297–98; Deacon 2013, 76–77). Thanks to random mutations, some descendants of these cells were sensitive to their environment and therefore had a survival advantage. In general, those that coped best lived long enough to transmit their genes. Among them, certain species of ape possessed traits that helped them get through epochs of drought. Among these species, there was one whose members tended to cooperate in large and complex groups (recall the evolutionary argument of Chapter 2). They were better able to hunt and forage together. At times when the groups of this species competed, an advantage fell to those that developed language (Tomasello 2014, 83, 95ff.). The members could explain things to one another in accordance with the regularities in their lives—for instance, they could give reasons for distributing food in a certain way. To understand the explanations, a member had to be able to adopt multiple perspectives. Arguments about reasons led to questions of principle beyond *ad hoc* issues. That is why we have Reason.

The existence of Reason, then, does not entail the existence of God. If natural selection can result in traits that enable the You-I Event, leading to joint attention, language, self-talk, and multiple perspectives, we need not haul in an already reasoning God to account for Reason.

***

In explaining conscience, desire, and reason, theism does a better job than materialism. But the two are not the sole alternatives. The account in this book is neither.

A truth re-enacted

Believers cannot be dissuaded by argument, because their relation with God re-enacts a truth long forgotten by the arguers on all sides. In my experience (for I once believed in God), during prayer one is given over to God and receives oneself. There is a feeling of fulfillment in those hours. Prayer is not self-talk: one does not play God toward oneself, but one does feel attended to.

This form of the You-I Event is expressed in Nicholas of Cusa's 15th-century *Vision of God*. Cusanus advises the reader to find a portrait-icon of Jesus in which the gaze seems to follow you as you move. Mount it on the wall, he writes, and then have a friend stand west of it while you stand to its east. Each will feel the gaze of the icon directed toward herself. To this he compares God's love:

> O Lord, Your seeing is loving; and just as Your gaze regards me so attentively that it never turns away from me, so neither does Your love ....
> Your Being, O Lord, does not forsake my being, for I exist insofar as You

are with me. And since Your seeing is Your being, *I exist because You look upon me*. And if You were to withdraw Your countenance from me, I would not at all continue to exist.[3]

(Hopkins 1985, 685; emphasis added)

That is as eloquent a description of the You-I Event as we have—but with one important difference. Unlike the carer in relation to an infant, the God of Cusanus never turns away. Assured that he will listen and respond, the grownup believer can let go of the secure self. Atheists may call faith infantile and God a projected parent, but behind the God of Cusanus stands the precluded You for whom even atheists yearn. It is a yearning for the You whom we miss—but do not know we miss—in flesh-and-blood encounters.

Does the fulfillment of that yearning continue beyond the time of prayer? Or is prayer a mere sample of the life we unconsciously miss? The test is in the intervals between prayers: do you talk to yourself?

After taking the roles of carers toward myself, I-the-child can violate relationships without endangering my awareness of my existence. If *sin* may be defined as the violation of relationships, then self-talk creates the structural basis for sin—it is, if you will, the original sin. Strangely though, it does not feel like sin at all. At the age when I begin to imitate adult speech, carers (at least in Western cultures) encourage it. They want me to become independent. They want me to be able to talk with myself, to "watch my tongue," be reflectively aware of myself, and control myself. By playing them toward myself in speech, I join my will to theirs. It is an anti-You conspiracy. Given their delight, I do not feel guilt, rather self-esteem.

On these terms, redemption from the original sin would be redemption *from* the restructured world of self-talk and *to* the You-I Event. *That* would be a Kingdom. But apart from the impossibility of such redemption, is it even desirable? To be fully human includes collective intentionality, and this requires self-talk (as said at the end of Chapter 4). The yearning for a You is part of being human, but there is nothing we can do to fulfill it.

If faith in God were miraculously to evaporate, the potential but precluded You would still be hidden in each encounter, a presence-in-absence pointing us toward each other.

---

3 I am indebted to F. Edward Cranz for hearing me out many years ago and pointing me to Cusanus.

14

What can be done

I have argued that the You-I Event is not rare for a baby. To explain why it becomes so, I have argued that the dread of separation motivates us to play the parts of carers toward ourselves in self-talk. But when its rarity is thus explained, the Event seems unattainable. One cannot talk oneself into not talking with oneself. Adepts in meditation may reach a state of inner silence, but it is doubtful whether they can long remain in it while interacting with someone.

Nonetheless, we have found openings through which the Event can *indirectly* enter our lives. In love, this happens with the growth of trust, on condition that the other's otherness is maintained. In work, the goal is often an avatar of the You. In art, a kind of You-I Event is aided by the fictive frame. In conversation, it is aided by the frame of the relationship. In religion, especially in prayer, the Event occurs directly, but with a spectral You in place of the true. Like a baby awaiting her absent carer, the split-off self remains active in us, scanning the world for openings.[1]

We cannot bring about You-I Events, but we can defend and widen the openings. Not all of them *should* be widened. I would not want to widen the opening afforded by a spectral You, nor that of a political cult. Even reading novels or seeing films can become addictive, distracting me from flesh-and-blood others. How then can we know which openings to widen and which to narrow? The criterion is the moral imperative: does the opening help us behave toward each human being as the You we fail to see?

The openings narrow or widen, depending on the social system. A system can conduce to more trust or less, lowering or raising the barrier of

---

1 I have said nothing of sports, hobbies, or politics. These can also serve as openings for limited You-I Events.

DOI: 10.4324/9781003543275-17

self-talk. A totalitarian police-state, dependent on informers, mews each up in herself. A capitalist democracy does not mew us up as much, but it cultivates self-interest, shaping us to compete. Already in 1905, Max Weber referred to "the technical and economic conditions of machine production which to-day determine the lives of all the individuals who are born into this mechanism, not only those directly concerned with economic acquisition, with irresistible force" (1958, 181).

A century after Weber, Ken Robinson reminded us that public educational systems originated to meet the needs of industrialism:

> In almost all industrial systems there is the same hierarchy of disciplines in high schools, and increasingly in elementary schools too. At the top are mathematics, languages and sciences .... There isn't a school system in the world that teaches dance every day as a compulsory discipline in the way that mathematics is taught (2011, 60) .... In many ways, the whole process of elementary and high school education is a protracted process of university entrance (p. 66) .... In many schools, students are educated from the waist up and attention eventually comes to focus on their heads, and particularly the left side (p. 117).
>
> (Robinson 2011)

If self-interest were the most basic human motive, capitalism would suit us to the core, while altruism and fellow-feeling would be products of socialization: skim them away and behold Lord Ego! But something else has been argued in this book. Deeper than Lord Ego is our rootedness in one another. Capitalism fits us, indeed, but only because of a change that sets in when I-the-child twist around as if I were you and address myself through your mask. As a result of the You-I account, I hope we can better understand self-interest: it is a counterfeit of basic connectedness.

In view of that connectedness, we can work toward a system that nourishes trust over mistrust, collaboration over competition.

I must qualify the word *trust*, because a superficial form of it impedes the You-I Event. Many are becoming personae on the World Wide Web. I trust you, stranger, because I know it is in your self-interest to get a good review from me. This is not the kind of trust on my part, or trustworthiness on yours, that lowers the threshold of dread. Big Brother is the quintessential mock You.

We need to cultivate the kind of trust that is intrinsic to relationship. Human beings naturally trust one another. We have a good reason: I am aware of my existence because, long ago, another person was trustworthy enough in attending to me. My trust in her was sometimes shaken, and the question of whether to trust or not became an issue in my relationships. But at the root of each encounter is the trust that developed in the first. We need a society that will nourish this elemental trust.

We do not have the luxury of designing a social system from scratch. We are in the midst of a new industrial revolution. Its outcome will transform our lives in ways that build trust or destroy it. Big pressures are tilting the balance toward destruction: climate change, the nuclear threat, cyberterrorism, genome editing, certain possibilities of artificial intelligence, unprecedented monopolies, technological unemployment, desperate migrations, racism, and extreme inequality. If collapse breeds chaos, the survivors may opt for fascism, which in digital form may outdo the worst that humans have known.

No matter how terrifying these prospects, we have the means to shape, as never before, a social system that will nourish elemental trust. In such a system, access to things will be less via ownership and more via sharing. Goods and services will be abundant and nearly free. Getting and spending will cease to lay waste our powers. Vertical structures of command and control (the legacy of the first two industrial revolutions) will diminish in importance, superseded by horizontally distributed, collaborative peer-to-peer networks, exemplified in open-source software (Rifkin 2014; Mason 2015; Raworth 2017). People will be free from the kinds of jobs that serve other people's projects instead of their own. Children will be educated less to compete and more to cooperate. In such a society, we will have time to cultivate the indirect openings. Despite the tempering of competition, humanity will advance, because the desire to learn and create is a form of yearning for the You.

Appendix

Replies to imagined critics

The You-I account faces several challenges. I have replied to the most obvious in the main text. Here are seven more with my responses.

***

Challenge 1: "It cannot be right to link a carer's attending with the baby's self-awareness. A second-trimester fetus shows signs of self-awareness, but she cannot feel attended to."

Reply: By the 22nd week of gestation, a fetus does indeed do things that indicate self-awareness. When reaching for this or that, she shapes her hand according to the nature of the target (Zoia et al. 2007). Also, *fetal twins* are sensitive to one another. From the 14th week, when Twin A reaches toward Twin B, she does so more slowly than when she reaches toward the uterine wall, her own mouth, or even her own eye, the most sensitive part of her body. These findings show a prenatal "propensity to socially oriented action" (Castiello et al. 2010, 1).

Let us suppose, then, that at a certain stage the fetus *is* self-aware. Would that nullify the You-I account? Not necessarily. Feminist phenomenologists (e.g., Sara Heinämaa) have claimed that the pregnant carer and the fetus are in a dynamic relationship (Heinämaa 2014). Beata Stawarska holds this to be the original form of Buber's I-You relationship, which is broken by birth, leaving us, she says, with a longing for the You as we once knew her (2009). Nicole Miglio writes:

> The impossibility for the gestating subject [the mother] to perceive the foetus as if it were only an object … is given by the free movements of the pre-infant, which can respond to movements, feelings, physiological changes, and psychological life of the maternal subject.
>
> (Miglio 2019, 85)

DOI: 10.4324/9781003543275-18

One might object that the experience of being attended to cannot exist for the fetus, since the requisite distance is lacking. Mere sensations, including kinesthesia, do not imply the existence of a person sensing them, nor do they betoken an external cause. In at least one kind of exchange, however, the fetus may feel attended to and respond. This was the suggestion of Viola Marx and Emese Nagy after studying twenty-three second- and third-trimester pregnancies:

> Overall results suggest that maternal touch of the abdomen was a powerful stimulus, producing a range of fetal behavioural responses. Fetuses displayed more arm, head, and mouth movements when the mother touched her abdomen as compared to maternal voice in situ.
>
> (Marx and Nagy 2015, 8)

Fetuses respond to touch on the mother's abdomen by the 21st week of gestation (earlier than previously thought). "[M]ost mothers and even fathers attempt to communicate with and regulate the behaviour of the fetus via stroking of the mother's abdomen *as a response* to the kicking or positional movements of the fetus." Citing the Zoia study on fetal reaching at 22 weeks, Marx and Nagy conclude: "[T]herefore it is plausible to suggest that the observed fetal responses to the voice and touch in the present study may have a communicative intent" (2015, 12; emphasis added).

If the You-I Event already occurs for the fetus, how do we explain the apparent awakening to social life that begins in the 2nd postnatal month and continues with carer-infant protoconversations? The first month may be a time of readjustment, in which the reciprocal touch of the prenatal period is replaced by the ostensive signals discussed in Chapter 2: eye contact, parentese, and turn-taking while feeding.

Studies of fetal experience are few, which is why I started with infancy. We can see, however, that the same principle may apply in both cases. Given an evolved disposition to feel attended to, fetal kicks and parental responses may suffice for a You-I Event.

***

Challenge 2: "Some babies get little or no attention but grow up to be self-aware."

Reply: The minimal amount of attention needed for survival will suffice to create self-awareness.

"But what about wild children, who were deserted at birth and survived? Do you claim they aren't self-aware?"

There is no firm evidence about "a putative wild child's life either before or during the period of isolation" (Saxe 2006).

A baby is biologically primed to meet a carer, and in cases of severe social deprivation, she can wait for a time without suffering permanent damage. In 20th-century Romanian orphanages, many babies had to wait too long. They had been brought there—most of them in their first few months—because their parents could not provide for them. We hear of two or three sharing a cot. In some institutions, the attendants did not feed them personally but propped the bottles. Here, then, is an extreme no-response situation, although the children could have responded to one another.

After the fall of Ceausescu in 1989, the orphanages were discovered by the rest of the world, and some babies were adopted. Jana Kreppner et al. (2007) studied those who had been adopted by couples in Britain and Canada. The children made progress, especially if they had spent less than six months in the orphanages. Most of the latter, on cognitive tests and tests of social attachment at the ages of 4, 6, and 11 years, ranked the same as adopted British children who had never been in orphanages. The developmental window had remained open during the first half year. Among those who had been in the orphanages longer than six months, most achieved typical social functioning after living in families, but a significant minority tended to attach themselves excessively and indiscriminately to anyone who came within range.

***

Challenge 3: "Autistic persons have a hard time connecting socially, but they are self-aware."

To elaborate on this challenge: Autism is said to include "persistent impairment in reciprocal social communication and social interaction" (American Psychiatric Association 2013). Yet autistic persons are aware of themselves. That seems discrepant with the You-I account.

Reply: Let it be admitted, first: "In the area of autism, the phenomenon is so complex and multifaceted that it's extremely difficult to find a single theory that explains everything" (Goldman 2006, 192).

Autism cannot be diagnosed until 18 months at the earliest, and many would say 3 years. No definitive biological marker has been found. Genes are a major factor, as determined in studies of twins, but the potentially relevant genes number in the hundreds. There is a method, nonetheless, by which the topic can be approached in early infancy. Because of the genetic factor, researchers can study babies with autistic relatives and then relate the results to those who are later diagnosed as autistic. Warren Jones and Ami Klin carried out an eye-tracking study with 110 infants, who watched a video of a woman apparently seeking to interact with them. At the age of 2 months (the starting age for the research), all made about the same amount of eye contact with her. However, for those who later received a diagnosis of autism, this age marked the beginning of a steady decline in such contact, and at 24 months they were making half as much as those who would prove to be neurotypical (W. Jones and Klin 2013). By the criterion of eye contact, then, autistic persons are not born with a problem of connecting socially (or the relevant genes are not yet expressed). Conceivably, they can experience You-I Events throughout infancy and toddlerhood. After that, furthermore, they continue to be emotionally attached to their principal carers (Teague et al. 2017). They need and seek romantic love. Since the early 1990s, many have been discovering one another on the Internet. "For all our cultural, political and neurological diversity, we found plenty in common, not only in the shared experience of trauma and marginalization but, for many of us, also in a certain fundamental autistic way of being" (Martijn Dekker in Fletcher-Watson and Happé 2019, 26).

An autistic child can also maintain self-awareness by making effects (on effects, see Chapter 3). In this regard, we should note a second diagnostic criterion: the autistic constellation is marked by "restricted, repetitive patterns of behavior, interests, or activities" (American Psychiatric Association 2013). These often take the form of making effects on one's own body or on things. To an autistic mind, however, such patterns may not seem repetitive or restrictive, rather islands of reliability in an unpredictable world. According to one group of researchers,

> some salient aspects of the autism phenotype may be manifestations of an underlying impairment in predictive abilities. With compromised prediction skills, an individual with autism inhabits a seemingly "magical" world wherein events occur unexpectedly and without cause. Immersion in such a capricious environment can prove overwhelming and compromise one's ability to effectively interact with it.
>
> (Sinha et al. 2014, 15220)

Other researchers had earlier suggested a way to explain the impaired prediction skills. Imaging brains with fMRI, they found that cortical responses to stimuli showed significantly more variation in "high-functioning" autistic persons compared with neurotypicals. As a result, there was more "noise" around each signal in the visual, auditory, and somatosensory cortices. The researchers speculate that

> unreliable neural activity early in development may create an unstable and unpredictable perception of the environment, which may be specifically accentuated in social situations that involve an added level of unpredictability (unlike objects, humans tend to exhibit variable behavior). Developing under such conditions might motivate an infant to retract from the environment, avoid social interaction, and focus instead on the performance of repetitive behaviors that generate more predictable neural responses.
>
> (Dinstein et al. 2012, 988)

In sum, the two main signs of autism may not reflect a social deficit, but even if they do, there are time and opportunity, in the first year, for a sense of self to develop.

***

Challenge 4: "If self-talk is the source of self-awareness after infancy, one would think it must be frequent, since we are self-aware when awake. Yet yet there are self-aware people who seldom engage in it."

To elaborate on this challenge: For decades Russell Hurlburt has been outfitting people with beepers that beep randomly during the day; at each beep, the subject jots down what was happening in her mind a microsecond earlier. A researcher then interviews the subject about the jottings. This method is called *Descriptive Experience Sampling* (DES). After training in it, the subjects become discriminating and exact in their responses. It turns out that on average, people are engaged in inner speech roughly one-fourth of the time before the beeps. Inner hearing is excluded from the count (Hurlburt et al. 2013).

Reply: As said in Chapter 4, I-the-child internalize other people by playing them toward myself in speech. I play some of them so often that they become *mock others*, always on tap. Attending to me innerly, they are part of me-as-subject in relation to external objects. Sometimes they address me, at other times they listen to me, but they can also attend in silence with me to things in the world. When Hurlburt conducts DES with people of school age or older, the method does not catch the periods of silent mock joint attention, which are just as effective as inner speech in keeping me aware of my existence.

Furthermore, in Chapter 5 we saw that work can be a derivative kind of You-I Event, enabling a kind of self-awareness and thereby suspending the compulsion to self-talk. Likewise, we saw in Chapter 8 that the enjoyment and making of art are also derived from the Event; art too enables a kind of self-awareness, hence a suspension of self-talk. In Chapter 9, we found a similar suspension when one listens to a lecture or converses. For most human beings, all these activities provide relief from self-talk within a world restructured by it.

***

Challenge 5: "The otherness of the other is vital to your theory, but infants do not understand that others see things differently. They are not fully aware of minds separate from their own."

Reply: In my infancy, your otherness consists largely in your freedom to attend to me or not. I cannot doubt your belief that I exist, for unless it is true there is no *me*. This infallibility of yours is generalized into the view that others cannot have false beliefs about anything (Southgate 2020). Discovering myself and my body through your responses, I know myself to be someone who smiles as you do, claps as you do, rejoices in the games you rejoice in, hence someone who, as an entity, is fundamentally like you. Based on the knowledge of my similarity to you, I initially assume that you know what I know. In the course of time, experience teaches me to curb this assumption. Already by 6 months, I know that your visual angle on a thing is different from mine (Luo and Johnson 2009). (Indeed, this much is implicit in the structure of the You-I Event.) But only after self-talk is established do I consider each of us to be an entity with an encapsulated mind—that is, a mind engaging in self-talk to which the other has no access. By my 4th or 5th year, I am free enough from the spell of the Event to understand that your beliefs may differ from what I know to be true.[1]

***

Challenge 6: "The account has a cultural bias."

To elaborate on this challenge: The You-I account is suited only to a modern Western urban industrial culture, which prioritizes personal

---

1 Based on looking-time experiments, some researchers claim that children much younger than 4 years also pass false-belief tests. For a review, see Scott and Baillargeon (2017). Others continue to hold that the turning point is at around age 4; see Powell et al. (2018).

independence over compliance to a group. In a culture stressing interdependence, as in the rural parts of Cameroon, there is much less face-to-face interaction at 3 months, compared with same-age dyads in a German city (Wörmann et al 2012). Or take a recently modernized culture like Japan; reciprocal smiling at 3 months is only a third as frequent as in the United States (Fogel et al. 1988).

Reply: To become aware of oneself, one does not need as much face-to-face (distal) attending as infants get in the West. In Chapter 2 we saw, with respect to rural Cameroon, that proximal attending through bodily contact will also do.

About Japan, the smiles last longer than in the United States, so there is not much difference in the total. After making the comparison, Alan Fogel confirmed "the universality of the face-to-face period in early infant development as a time when parent and infant communicate primarily affective information without the mediation of objects or other persons" (Fogel et al. 1988, 405).

Surveying studies of cultural differences in parenting, Michael Tomasello concludes: "[D]espite these cultural differences in *adult* behavior, as far as we know infants' skills in protoconversation are similar in all cultures." The same holds for joint attention: "[I]n many traditional cultures parents almost never play with young infants around objects, mainly because adults have little free time …. Nevertheless …, as far as we know, infants' skills in joint attention are similar in all cultures" (Tomasello 2019, 62–63).

***

Challenge 7: "You restrict your discussion to dyadic relations."

To elaborate on this challenge: The You-I account attracts a criticism against Freud made by Barbara Ehrenreich in her book about collective joy:

> In Freud's scheme of human affinities, there was only one kind of love: the dyadic, erotic love of one individual for another …. Freud could not imagine a kind of love binding … larger groups of persons. Eros, he said, could unite people two by two …. Hence the excitement of groups could only be derivative of the individuals' dyadic love for the group leader; never mind that ecstatic groups, of the kind observed in "primitive" ritual, often had no leader or central figure at all.
>
> (Ehrenreich 2007, 23)

Reply: When Ehrenreich speaks of the dyad, I gather that she thinks of it as existing alongside other dyads, triads, and larger groupings within a wider world. She takes a bird's eye view on these. In the You-I account, we restrict ourselves initially to the viewpoint of the child, imagining it with the help of research. When the baby and carer engage in joint attention to a third thing or person, this is not just a shift from dyadic to triadic relations. Rather, as said in Chapter 4, the mutuality between self and other expands to involve other "topics" (Reddy 2009, 102).[2]

Returning to leaderless, collective joy: Historian William McNeill discusses basic training during World War II. His unit was waiting for weapons, and the soldiers spent much of the day just marching in close formation on the drill field. After weeks of this, when they had achieved a degree of synchrony, McNeill began to have an unusual feeling:

> Words are inadequate to describe the emotion aroused by the prolonged movement in unison that drilling involved. A sense of pervasive well-being is what I recall; more specifically, a strange sense of personal enlargement; a sort of swelling out, becoming bigger than life, thanks to participation in collective ritual. ... [It was] a state of generalized emotional exaltation whose warmth was indubitable, without, however, having any definite external meaning or attachment ....
>
> Obviously, something visceral was at work; something, I later concluded, far older than language and critically important in human history, because the emotion it arouses constitutes an indefinitely expansible basis for social cohesion among any and every group that keeps together in time, moving big muscles together and chanting, singing, or shouting rhythmically.
>
> (McNeill 1995, 2)

Both the group trance-dance and military drilling take place in frames. Ehrenreich points out that the former

> was in fact deliberately planned, organized, and at all times subject to cultural rules and expectations .... Appropriate foods had to be gathered

---

2 Conceivably the You can be plural, as when a baby engages with both parents at once. See Fivaz-Depeursinge et al. (2004).

and prepared in advance; costumes and masks designed; songs and dances rehearsed …. Furthermore, even at the height of the supposed frenzy, cultural expectations guided behavior, determining the special roles of the sexes and age groups, and going so far as to regulate that "wildest" of experiences—trance.

(Ehrenreich 2007, 25)

It is an unusual kind of framing. In the examples I gave in Chapter 8 on art, I talked of a division between the self that enters the frame and the self that remains in reserve outside. But in the examples of group dancing and military drilling, a person rehearses until she no longer needs to be conscious of herself as a unit performing the steps; after that point, when she enters the dance, she leaves her everyday self without reserve, relying on the group's tradition. In my terms, it is the secure self that she leaves behind. She entrusts herself to the frame. Unlike the viewer of art, or the audience at a play, or the reader of a novel, she lets go of the rim and gives herself over, trusting that tradition will prevail and the drumming finally stop.

Acknowledgments

I owe much to talks with Vasudevi Reddy. Her challenges led me to sharpen my thought about what happens when infant and caregiver attend to one another.

I also owe many refinements to the editors and anonymous reviewers of my articles, in which I tested the You-I account. The journals, fully cited in the References, are *Phenomenology and the Cognitive Sciences* (edited by Shaun Gallagher and Dan Zahavi, 2012), *Journal of Theoretical and Philosophical Psychology* (edited by Jeff Sugarman, 2014), *Journal of Phenomenological Psychology* (edited by James Morley, 2016), *Human Studies* (edited by Martin Endress, 2018), and *Journal of Consciousness Studies* (edited by Graham Horswell, 2023).

My thanks go out to Jon Mills, editor of the Routledge series, Philosophy & Psychoanalysis, in which this work appears. Responding to a query of mine, Dr. Mills suggested that I submit the proposal that has led to publication.

Philosophy Meets the Infant has been fifteen years in the writing. Professors Ted Estess and W. F. "Bill" Monroe, as well as freelance editor Nancy Mangum McCaslin, responded to parts of it at all stages. Dr. Dan Price brought his philosophical acuity to bear on the first draft. A decade later, Stefano Vincini engaged with me on Husserl's theory of pairing.

Close to the finish, I expounded my ideas over Provençal wine to Sigune Kröger and Wolfram Jäger. Dr. Jäger then read the full draft of the book, commented incisively, and translated the first chapter into German for discussion among friends.

At various stages, I also received helpful comments from Raphaël Du Bosch, Johannes Fischer, Larry George, Sabrina George, Judy and Bob Goldman, Reinhard Guischard, Andrea Heggen, Marcus Kleinert, Mark

Leifeste, Jennifer Lile, Chris Maher, Leora Sotto, Elizabeth Whalley, John Windle, and Dr. Jim Wise.

I am grateful to Routledge's Katie Randall, Manon Berset, and Niamh Hitchmough for quick and generous responses to my many queries. I also thank Vinodhini Kumaran, Project Manager at codeMantra, for her promptness, attention to detail, and boundless care.

My daughter Talya Langfur has read the book several times over the many years, commenting from her experience as a physical therapist with children. She has been my uncompromising critic, mainstay, and all the good things one cannot name because they developed at a time before language.

The time before language is reflected in the section on music, inspired by my son Benny Langfur.

My partner, Roni Ben Efrat, sustains me.

References

Ainsworth, Mary D. Salter, Silvia M. Bell, and Donelda J. Stayton. 1972. "Individual Differences in the Development of Some Attachment Behaviors." *Merrill-Palmer Quarterly of Behavior and Development* 18 (2): 123–43.

American Psychiatric Association. 2013. *Diagnostic and Statistical Manual of Mental Disorders (DSM-5®)*. Arlington, VA: American Psychiatric Publishing.

Arain, Mariam, Maliha Haque, Lina Johal, Puja Mathur, Wynand Nel, Afsha Rais, Ranbir Sandhu, and Sushil Sharma. 2013. "Maturation of the Adolescent Brain." *Neuropsychiatric Disease and Treatment* 9: 449–61. https://doi.org/10.2147/NDT.S39776.

Astor, Kim, Maleen Thiele, and Gustaf Gredebäck. 2021. "Gaze Following Emergence Relies on Both Perceptual Cues and Social Awareness." *Cognitive Development* 60: 101121. https://doi.org/10.1016/j.cogdev.2021.101121.

Baars, Bernard J. 1997. *In the Theater of Consciousness: The Workspace of the Mind*. New York: Oxford University Press.

Badiou, Alain. 2009. *In Praise of Love*. Translated by Peter Bush. Paris: Flammarion SA.

Balsam, Rosemary H. 2010. "Where Has Oedipus Gone? A Turn of the Century Contemplation." *Psychoanalytic Inquiry* 30 (6): 511–19. https://doi.org/10.1080/07351690.2010.518532.

Beauvoir, Simone de. 1956. *The Second Sex*. Translated by Harvard Madison Parshley. London: Jonathan Cape.

Bermúdez, José Luis. 2000. *The Paradox of Self-Consciousness*. Cambridge: MIT Press.

Bertenthal, Bennett I., and James L. Rose. 1995. "Two Modes of Perceiving the Self." In *The Self in Infancy: Theory and Research*, edited by Philippe Rochat, 112: 303–26. Amsterdam: Elsevier Science B. V.

Bigelow, Ann E. 1995. "The Effect of Blindness on the Early Development of the Self." In *The Self in Infancy: Theory and Research*, edited by Philippe Rochat, 327–47. Amsterdam: Elsevier Science B. V.

Bigelow, Ann E., and Michelle Power. 2016. "Effect of Maternal Responsiveness on Young Infants' Social Bidding-like Behavior during the Still Face Task." *Infant and Child Development* 25 (3): 256–76. https://doi.org/10.1111/infa.12221.

Bigelow, Ann E., and Philippe Rochat. 2006. "Two-month-old Infants' Sensitivity to Social Contingency in Mother–Infant and Stranger–Infant Interaction." *Infancy* 9 (3): 313–25.

Bloom, Paul. 2013. *Just Babies: The Origins of Good and Evil*. New York: Crown Publishers.

Booth, Wayne. C. 1983. *The Rhetoric of Fiction*. 2nd ed. Chicago, IL: University of Chicago Press.

Booth, Wayne. C. 1998. "Why Banning Ethical Criticism Is a Serious Mistake." *Philosophy and Literature* 22 (2): 366–93. https://doi.org/10.1353/phl. 1998.0029.

Bowlby, John. 1960. "Separation Anxiety." *The International Journal of Psycho-Analysis* XLI: 89–113.

Brandt, Anthony, Molly Gebrian, and L. Robert Slevc. 2012. "Music and Early Language Acquisition." *Frontiers in Psychology* 3. https://doi.org/10.3389/fpsyg.2012.00327.

Bråten, Stein. 2009. *The Intersubjective Mirror in Infant Learning and Evolution of Speech*. Amsterdam: John Benjamins Pub.

Brown, Norman O. 1959. *Life Against Death: The Psychoanalytical Meaning of History*. New York: Vintage.

Buber, Martin. 1971/1929. "Dialogue." *Between Man and Man*. Translated by Ronald Gregor Smith. New York: Macmillan.

Buber, Martin. 1995/1923. *Ich und Du*. Stuttgart: Philipp Reclam.

Campanella, Jennifer, and Carolyn Rovee-Collier. 2005. "Latent Learning and Deferred Imitation at 3 Months." *Infancy* 7 (3): 243–62. https://doi.org/10.1207/s15327078in0703_2.

Castiello, Umberto, Cristina Becchio, Stefania Zoia, Cristian Nelini, Luisa Sartori, Laura Blason, Giuseppina D'Ottavio, Maria Bulgheroni, and Vittorio Gallese. 2010. "Wired to Be Social: The Ontogeny of Human Interaction." *PLoS One* 5 (10): e13199.

Cavell, Marcia. 2006. *Becoming a Subject: Reflections in Philosophy and Psychoanalysis*. Oxford: Clarendon Press.

Chodorow, Nancy. 1978. "Mothering, Object-Relations, and the Female Oedipal Configuration." *Feminist Studies* 4 (1): 137–58.

Christoff, Kalina, Alan M. Gordon, Jonathan Smallwood, Rachelle Smith, and Jonathan W. Schooler. 2009. "Experience Sampling during fMRI Reveals Default Network and Executive System Contributions to Mind Wandering." *Proceedings of the National Academy of Sciences* 106 (21): 8719–24.

Clark, Timothy J. 2013. *Picasso and Truth: From Cubism to Guernica*. Vol. 58. A. W. Mellon Lectures in the Fine Arts. Princeton, NJ: Princeton University Press.

Cooper, Robin Panneton, and Richard N. Aslin. 1990. "Preference for Infant-Directed Speech in the First Month after Birth." *Child Development* 61 (5): 1584. https://doi.org/10.2307/1130766.

Cox, Brian, and Andrew Cohen. 2015. *Human Universe*. London: William Collins.

Csibra, Gergely. 2010. "Recognizing Communicative Intentions in Infancy." *Mind & Language* 25 (2): 141–68. https://doi.org/10.1111/j.1468-0017.2009.01384.x.

Davidson, Janet E. 2003. "Insights about Insightful Problem Solving." In *The Psychology of Problem Solving*, edited by Janet E. Davidson and Robert J. Sternberg, 149–75. New York: Cambridge University Press.

Deacon, Terrence W. 1998. *The Symbolic Species: The Co-Evolution of Language and the Brain.* New York: WW Norton & Company.

Deacon, Terrence W. 2013. *Incomplete Nature: How Mind Emerged from Matter.* New York: W.W. Norton & Company.

Dinstein, Ilan, David J. Heeger, Lauren Lorenzi, Nancy J. Minshew, Rafael Malach, and Marlene Behrmann. 2012. "Unreliable Evoked Responses in Autism." *Neuron* 75 (6): 981–91. https://doi.org/10.1016/j.neuron.2012.07.026.

Dore, John. 1989. "Monologue as Reenvoicement of Dialogue." In *Narratives from the Crib*, edited by Katherine Nelson, 231–60. Cambridge, MA: Harvard University Press.

Dowden, Edward. 1887. *Studies in Literature 1789–1877.* 3rd ed. London: Kegan Paul, Trench.

Dunbar, Robin. 2014. *Human Evolution: A Pelican Introduction.* London: Penguin.

Duncan, Robert, and Donato Tarulli. 2009. "On the Persistence of Private Speech: Empirical and Theoretical Considerations." In *Private Speech, Executive Functioning, and the Development of Verbal Self-Regulation*, edited by Adam Winsler, Charles Fernyhough, and Ignacio Montero. Cambridge University Press. https://psycnet.apa.org/doi/10.1017/CBO9780511581533.015.

Eckardt, Alice L. 1994. *Suffering: Challenge to Faith, Challenge to God.* Bethlehem, PA: Lehigh University Faculty Publications. https://preserve.lehigh.edu/cas-religion-faculty-publications/12.

Ehrenreich, Barbara. 2007. *Dancing in the Streets: A History of Collective Joy.* New York: Macmillan.

Eliot, George. 1911/1871–1872. *Middlemarch.* Vol. 1. New York: Thomas Nelson.

Erikson, Erik. 1963. *Childhood and Society.* New York: Norton.

Fagard, Jaqueline, Rana Esseily, Lisa Jacquey, Kevin O'Regan, and Eszter Somogyi. 2018. "Fetal Origin of Sensorimotor Behavior." *Frontiers in Neurorobotics* 12 (May): 23. https://doi.org/10.3389/fnbot.2018.00023.

Farroni, Teresa, Gergely Csibra, Francesca Simion, and Mark H. Johnson. 2002. "Eye Contact Detection in Humans from Birth." *Proceedings of the National Academy of Sciences* 99 (14): 9602–05. https://www.pnas.org/cgi/doi/10.1073/pnas.152159999.

Farroni, Teresa, Stefano Massaccesi, Donatella Pividori, and Mark H. Johnson. 2004. "Gaze Following in Newborns." *Infancy* 5 (1): 39–60. https://doi.org/10.1207/s15327078in0501_2.

Fernald, Anne. 1985. "Four-Month-Old Infants Prefer to Listen to Motherese." *Infant Behavior and Development* 8 (2): 181–95. https://doi.org/10.1016/S0163-6383(85)80005-9.

Fernyhough, Charles. 2016. *The Voices Within: The History and Science of How We Talk to Ourselves*. Kindle. London: Profile Books.

Feuerbach, Ludwig. 1981/1843. *Grundsätze der Philosophie der Zukunft. Gesammelte Werke, Band 9, 1981–*. Berlin: De Gruyter.

Fivaz-Depeursinge, Elisabeth, Nicholas Favez, and France Frascarolo. 2004. "Threesome Intersubjectivity in Infancy." In *The Structure and Development of Self-Consciousness: Interdisciplinary Perspectives*, edited by Dan Zahavi, Thor Grünbaum, and Josef Parnas, 21–34. Amsterdam: John Benjamins.

Fletcher-Watson, Sue, and Francesca Happé. 2019. *Autism: A New Introduction to Psychological Theory and Current Debate*. New York: Routledge.

Fogel, Alan, Sueko Toda, and Masatoshi Kawai. 1988. "Mother-Infant Face-to-Face Interaction in Japan and the United States: A Laboratory Comparison Using 3-Month-Old Infants." *Developmental Psychology* 24 (3): 398–406. https://doi.org/10.1037/0012-1649.24.3.398.

Fonagy, Peter, George Gergely, and Mary Target. 2007. "The Parent-Infant Dyad and the Construction of the Subjective Self." *Journal of Child Psychology and Psychiatry* 48 (3–4): 288–328. https://doi.org/10.1111/j.1469-7610.2007.01727.x.

Freud, Sigmund. 1955/1922. "The Medusa's Head." In *Beyond the Pleasure Principle, Group Psychology and Other Works (1920–1922)*, translated and edited by James Strachey, The Standard Edition of the Complete Psychological Works of Sigmund Freud, XVIII: 273–74. London: The Hogarth Press and the Institute of Psycho-Analysis.

Freud, Sigmund. 1961/1923. "The Ego and the Id." In *The Ego and the Id and Other Works*, translated by James Strachey, The Standard Edition of the Complete Psychological Works of Sigmund Freud, XIX: 3–66. London: The Hogarth Press and the Institute of Psycho-Analysis.

Freud, Sigmund. 1964/1933. *New Introductory Lectures on Psycho-Analysis and Other Works (1932–1936)*. Translated by James Strachey. The Standard Edition of the Complete Psychological Works of Sigmund Freud. Vol. XXI. London: The Hogarth Press and the Institute of Psycho-Analysis.

Freud, Sigmund. 1991/1900. *The Interpretation of Dreams*. Translated by James Strachey. London: Penguin.

Gabbard, Glen O. 2016. *Boundaries and Boundary Violations in Psychoanalysis*. 2nd ed. Arlington, VA: American Psychiatric Association Publishing.

Gerhardt, Julie. 1989. "Monologue as a Speech Genre." In *Narratives from the Crib*, edited by Katherine Nelson, 171–230. Cambridge, MA: Harvard University Press.

Gibson, James J. 2015. *The Ecological Approach to Visual Perception*. New York: Psychology Press.

Gibson, Walker. 1950. "Authors, Speakers, Readers, and Mock Readers." *College English* 11 (5): 265. https://doi.org/10.2307/585994.

Gil-White, Francisco J. 2001. "Are Ethnic Groups Biological 'Species' to the Human Brain?: Essentialism in Our Cognition of Some Social Categories." *Current Anthropology* 42 (4): 515–53. https://doi.org/10.1086/321802.

Glatzer, Nahum N., ed. 1961. *Franz Rosenzweig: His Life and Thought*. New York: Schocken Books.

Goldin-Meadow, Susan. 2003. *Hearing Gesture: How Our Hands Help Us Think*. Cambridge, MA: Harvard University Press.

Goldman, Alvin I. 2006. *Simulating Minds: The Philosophy, Psychology, and Neuroscience of Mindreading*. New York: Oxford University Press.

Gopnik, Alison. 2009. *The Philosophical Baby: What Children's Minds Tell Us about Truth, Love & the Meaning of Life*. New York: Farrar, Straus and Giroux. Kindle Edition.

Greenberg, Irving. 1977. "Cloud of Smoke, Pillar of Fire: Judaism, Christianity, and Modernity after the Holocaust." In *Auschwitz: Beginning of a New Era?*, edited by Eva Fleischner, 7–55. Brooklyn, NT: KTAV.

Haidt, Jonathan. 2012. *The Righteous Mind: Why Good People Are Divided by Politics and Religion*. Kindle. New York: Knopf Doubleday Publishing Group.

Hart, David Bentley. 2005. *The Doors of the Sea: Where Was God in the Tsunami?* Grand Rapids, MI: Wm. B. Eerdmans Publishing.

Heidegger, Martin. 1967/1927. *Sein und Zeit [Being and Time]*. 11th ed. Tübingen: Niemeyer.

Heidegger, Martin. 1988/1927. *The Basic Problems of Phenomenology*. Translated by Albert Hofstadter. Bloomington: Indiana University Press. Kindle Edition.

Heinämaa, Sara. 2014. "'An Equivocal Couple Overwhelmed by Life': A Phenomenological Analysis of Pregnancy." *Philosophia* 4 (1): 31–49.

Hendin, Herbert, and Ann Pollinger Haas. 1991. "Suicide and Guilt as Manifestations of PTSD in Vietnam Combat Veterans." *American Journal of Psychiatry* 148 (5): 586–91. https://doi.org/10.1176/ajp.148.5.586.

Henrich, Dieter. 2003. *Between Kant and Hegel: Lectures on German Idealism*. Edited by David S. Pacini. Cambridge, MA: Harvard University Press.

Hermans, Hubert J. M. 2004. "The Dialogical Self: Between Exchange and Power." In *The Dialogical Self in Psychotherapy: An Introduction*, edited by Hubert J. M. Hermans and Giancarlo Dimaggio, 13–28. New York: Brunner-Routledge.

Hood, Bruce M., J. Douglas Willen, and Jon Driver. 1998. "Adult's Eyes Trigger Shifts of Visual Attention in Human Infants." *Psychological Science* 9 (2): 131–34. https://doi.org/10.1111/1467-9280.00024.

Hopkins, Jasper. 1985. *Nicholas of Cusa's Dialectical Mysticism: Text, Translation, and Interpretive Study of De Visione Dei*. Minneapolis, MN: Arthur J. Banning.

Horney, Karen. 2019. "The Flight from Womanhood: The Masculinity-Complex in Women, as Viewed by Men and Women." In *Female Sexuality*, edited by Russell Grigg, Dominique Hecq, and Craig Smith, 107–21. London: Routledge. https://doi.org/10.4324/9780429474675.

Hrdy, Sarah Blaffer. 2009. *Mothers and Others: The Evolutionary Origins of Mutual Understanding*. Cambridge, MA: Harvard University Press.

Hrdy, Sarah Blaffer, and Judith M. Burkart. 2020. "The Emergence of Emotionally Modern Humans: Implications for Language and Learning." *Philosophical Transactions of the Royal Society B: Biological Sciences* 375 (1803): 20190499. https://doi.org/10.1098/rstb.2019.0499.

Hurlburt, Russell T., Christopher L. Heavey, and Jason M. Kelsey. 2013. "Toward a Phenomenology of Inner Speaking." *Consciousness and Cognition* 22 (4): 1477–94. https://doi.org/10.1016/j.concog.2013.10.003.

Husserl, Edmund. 1960/1929. *Cartesian Meditations: An Introduction to Phenomenology*. Translated by Dorion Cairns. The Hague: Martinus Nijhoff.

Husserl, Edmund. 1989/1952. *Ideas Pertaining to a Pure Phenomenology and to a Phenomenological Philosophy, Second Book: Studies in the Phenomenology of Constitution*. Translated by Richard Rojcewicz and André Schuwer. Dordrecht: Kluwer Academic.

Husserl, Edmund. 1991/1893–1917. *On the Phenomenology of the Consciousness of Internal Time*. Translated by John B. Brough. Dordrecht: Kluwer Academic.

Husserl, Edmund. 2006/1929–1934. *Späte Texte über Zeitkonstitution (1929–1934): Die C-Manuskripte*. Dordrecht: Springer.

Irigaray, Luce. 1985. *Speculum of the Other Woman*. Translated by Gillian C. Gill. Ithaca, NY: Cornell University Press.

Jones, James M., John F. Dovidio, and Deborah L. Vietze. 2013. *The Psychology of Diversity: Beyond Prejudice and Racism*. Oxford: Wiley Blackwell.

Jones, Warren, and Ami Klin. 2013. "Attention to Eyes Is Present but in Decline in 2–6-Month-Old Infants Later Diagnosed with Autism." *Nature* 504 (7480): 427–31. https://doi.org/10.1038/nature12715.

Jonsson, Carl-Otto, and David Clinton. 2006. "What do Mothers Attune to during Interactions with their Infants?" *Infant and Child Development* 15 (4): 387–402. https://doi.org/10.1002/icd.466.

Jouen, François, Jean-Claude Lepecq, Olivier Gapenne, and Bennett I. Bertenthal. 2000. "Optic Flow Sensitivity in Neonates." *Infant Behavior and Development* 23 (3–4): 271–84.

Kafka, Franz. 1977/1959. *Letters to Friends, Family, and Editors*. Translated by Richard Winston and Clara Winston. New York: Schocken Books.

Kafka, Franz. 2017/1931. *Betrachtungen über Sünde, Leid, Hoffnung und den wahren Weg*. Munich: BookRix.

Kant, Immanuel. 2002/1804. "What Real Progress Has Metaphysics Made in Germany since the Time of Leibniz and Wolff?" In *Immanuel Kant: Theoretical Philosophy after 1781*, edited by Henry Allison and Peter Heath, translated by Henry Allison, 337–424. New York: Cambridge University Press.

Kant, Immanuel. 2005/1785. *Groundwork for the Metaphysics of Morals*. Edited by Lara Denis. Translated by Thomas K. Abbott and Lara Denis. Orchard Park, NY: Broadview.

Kärtner, Joscha, Heidi Keller, and Relindis D. Yovsi. 2010. "Mother-Infant Interaction during the first 3 Months: The Emergence of Culture-Specific Contingency Patterns." *Child Development* 81 (2): 540–54. https://doi.org/10.1111/j.1467-8624.2009.01414.x.

Kaye, Kenneth. 1977. "Toward the Origin of Dialogue." In *Studies in Mother-Infant Interaction*, edited by H. Rudolph Schaffer, 89–117. London: Academic Press.

Kaye, Kenneth, and Anne J. Wells. 1980. "Mothers' Jiggling and the Burst-Pause Pattern in Neonatal Feeding." *Infant Behavior and Development* 3: 29–46.

Keller, Helen. 1903. *The Story of My Life: With Her Letters (1887–1901) and a Supplementary Account of Her Education, Including Passages from the Reports and Letters of Her Teacher, Anne Mansfield Sullivan by John Albert Macy*. New York: Doubleday, Page and Co.

Kenny, Dianna T. 2013. *Bringing up Baby: The Psychoanalytic Infant Comes of Age*. London: Karnac.

Kierkegaard, Søren. 1960/1846. *Kierkegaard's Concluding Unscientific Postscript*. Translated by David Swenson and Walter Lowrie. Princeton, NJ: Princeton University Press.

Kleeman, James A. 1966. "Genital Self-Discovery during a Boy's Second Year: A Follow-Up." *The Psychoanalytic Study of the Child* 21 (1): 358–92. https://doi.org/10.1080/00797308.1966.11823264.

Kleeman, James A. 1967. "The Peek-A-Boo Game." *The Psychoanalytic Study of the Child* 22 (1): 239–73. https://doi.org/10.1080/00797308.1967.11822599.

Klein, Melanie. 1946. "Notes on Some Schizoid Mechanisms." *International Journal of Psycho-Analysis* 27: 99–110.

Kobayashi, Hiromi, and Shiro Kohshima. 2001. "Unique Morphology of the Human Eye and Its Adaptive Meaning: Comparative Studies on External Morphology of the Primate Eye." *Journal of Human Evolution* 40 (5): 419–35. https://doi.org/10.1006/jhev.2001.0468.

Kohut, Heinz. 1971. *The Analysis of the Self*. Chicago, IL: University of Chicago Press. Kindle Edition.

Kohut, Heinz. 1977. *The Restoration of the Self*. Chicago, IL: University of Chicago Press. Kindle Edition.

Kosslyn, Stephen M., William L. Thompson, and Giorgio Ganis. 2006. *The Case for Mental Imagery*. Oxford: Oxford University Press. Kindle Edition.

Køster, Allan. 2021. "The Felt Sense of the Other: Contours of a Sensorium." *Phenomenology and the Cognitive Sciences* 20 (1): 57–73. https://doi.org/10.1007/s11097-020-09657-3.

Kreppner, Jana M., Michael Rutter, Celia Beckett, Jenny Castle, Emma Colvert, Christine Groothues, Amanda Hawkins, Thomas G. O'Connor, Suzanne Stevens, and Edmund J. S. Sonuga-Barke. 2007. "Normality and Impairment Following Profound Early Institutional Deprivation: A Longitudinal Follow-up into Early Adolescence." *Developmental Psychology* 43 (4): 931–46. https://doi.org/10.1037/0012-1649.43.4.931.

Kurzban, Robert, John Tooby, and Leda Cosmides. 2001. "Can Race Be Erased? Coalitional Computation and Social Categorization." *Proceedings of the National Academy of Sciences* 98 (26): 15387–92. https://doi.org/10.1073/pnas.251541498.

Kushner, Harold S. 1981. *When Bad Things Happen to Good People.* Kindle. New York: Anchor.

Langfur, Stephen. 2013. "The You-I Event: On the Genesis of Self-Awareness." *Phenomenology and the Cognitive Sciences* 12 (4): 769–90. https://doi.org/10.1007/s11097-012-9282-y.

Langfur, Stephen. 2014. "Heidegger and the Infant: A Second-Person Alternative to the Dasein-Analysis." *Journal of Theoretical and Philosophical Psychology* 34 (4): 257–74. https://doi.org/10.1037/a0038004.

Langfur, Stephen. 2016. "The Interactive Now: A Second-Person Approach to Time-Consciousness." *Journal of Phenomenological Psychology* 47 (2): 156–82. https://doi.org/10.1163/15691624-12341312.

Langfur, Stephen. 2019. "Cogitor Ergo Sum: The Origin of Self-Awareness in Dyadic Interaction." *Human Studies* 42 (3): 425–50. https://doi.org/10.1007/s10746-018-09487-y.

Langfur, Stephen. 2023. "Locating the 'Inner'." *Journal of Consciousness Studies* 30 (1–2): 191–214. https://doi.org/10.53765/20512201.30.1.191.

Langfur, Stephen. 2023/1992. *Confession from a Jericho Jail.* 2nd ed. Burlington, VT: Fomite Press.

Lavelli, Manuela, and Marco Poli. 1998. "Early Mother-Infant Interaction during Breast- and Bottle-Feeding." *Infant Behavior and Development* 21 (4): 667–83. https://doi.org/10.1016/S0163-6383(98)90037-6.

Leont'ev, Aleksei N. 1981. "The Problem of Activity in Psychology." In *The Concept of Activity in Soviet Psychology*, edited and translated by James V. Wertsch, 37–71. Armonk, NY: M. E. Sharpe, Inc.

Lewis, C. S. 1967. *Miracles.* London: HarperCollins.

Lewis, C. S. 1977. *The Pilgrim's Regress.* London: Fount.

Lewis, C. S. 2001/1952. *Mere Christianity.* London: HarperCollins.

Libet, Benjamin. 1985. "Unconscious Cerebral Initiative and the Role of Conscious Will in Voluntary Action." *Behavioral and Brain Sciences* 8 (4): 529–39. https://doi.org/10.1017/S0140525X00044903.

Linden, David J. 2012. *The Accidental Mind.* Kindle. Cambridge, MA: Harvard University Press.

Luo, Yuyan, and Susan C. Johnson. 2009. "Recognizing the Role of Perception in Action at 6 Months." *Developmental Science* 12 (1): 142–49. https://doi.org/10.1111/j.1467-7687.2008.00741.x.

Maguen, Shira, Thomas J. Metzler, Brett T. Litz, Karen H. Seal, Sara J. Knight, and Charles R. Marmar. 2009. "The Impact of Killing in War on Mental Health Symptoms and Related Functioning." *Journal of Traumatic Stress* 22 (5): 435–43. https://doi.org/10.1002/jts.20451.

Malloch, Stephen N. 1999. "Mothers and Infants and Communicative Musicality." *Musicae Scientiae* 3 (1_suppl): 29–57. https://doi.org/10.1177/10298649000030S104.

Mann, Thomas. 1924. *Der Zauberberg.* Berlin: S. Fischer.

Maoz, Uri, Gideon Yaffe, Christof Koch, and Liad Mudrik. 2019. "Neural Precursors of Decisions That Matter—An ERP Study of Deliberate and Arbitrary Choice." *Elife* 8: e39787. https://doi.org/10.7554/eLife.39787.

Marx, Viola, and Emese Nagy. 2015. "Fetal Behavioural Responses to Maternal Voice and Touch," edited by Pier Francesco Ferrari. *PLoS One* 10 (6): e0129118. https://doi.org/10.1371/journal.pone.0129118.

Masataka, Nobuo. 2003. *The Onset of Language*. New York: Cambridge University Press.

McNeill, William H. 1995. *Keeping Together in Time: Dance and Drill in Human History*. Cambridge, MA: Harvard University Press.

Mason, Paul. 2015. *Postcapitalism: A Guide to Our Future*. New York: Farrar, Straus and Giroux.

Mead, George Herbert. 1967. *Mind, Self, and Society*. Chicago, IL: The University of Chicago Press.

Meltzoff, Andrew N., and M. Keith Moore. 1994. "Imitation, Memory, and the Representation of Persons." *Infant Behavior and Development* 17: 83–99. https://doi.org/10.1016%2F0163-6383(94)90024-8.

Mensch, James R. 2010. *Husserl's Account of Our Consciousness of Time*. Milwaukee: Marquette University Press.

Miglio, Nicole. 2019. "Affective Schemas, Gestational Incorporation, and Fetal-Maternal Touch: A Husserlian Inquiry." *HUMANA. MENTE Journal of Philosophical Studies* 12 (36): 67–99.

Mills, Jon. 2016. *Inventing God: Psychology of Belief and the Rise of Secular Spirituality*. London: Routledge.

Minter, David. 1994. "Faulkner, Childhood, and the Making of *The Sound and the Fury*." In *The Sound and the Fury: An Authoritative Text*, edited by David Minter, Norton Critical Editions, 343–58. New York: Norton.

Mitchell, Kevin J. 2023. *Free Agents: How Evolution Gave Us Free Will*. Princeton, NJ: Princeton University Press.

Moguillansky, Carlos, and Howard B. Levine. 2022. *Psychoanalysis of the Psychoanalytic Frame Revisited: A New Look at José Bleger's Classic Work*. New York: Taylor & Francis.

Moll, Henrike, and Michael Tomasello. 2007. "Cooperation and Human Cognition: The Vygotskian Intelligence Hypothesis." *Philosophical Transactions of the Royal Society B: Biological Sciences* 362 (1480): 639–48. https://doi.org/10.1098/rstb.2006.2000.

Murray, Lynne, Leonardo De Pascalis, Laura Bozicevic, Laura Hawkins, Valentina Sclafani, and Pier Francesco Ferrari. 2016. "The Functional Architecture of Mother-Infant Communication, and the Development of Infant Social Expressiveness in the First Two Months." *Scientific Reports* 6 (1): 39019. https://doi.org/10.1038/srep39019.

Nelson, Katherine, ed. 1989. *Narratives from the Crib*. Cambridge, MA: Harvard University Press.

Nguyen, Trinh, Drew H. Abney, Dina Salamander, Bennett I. Bertenthal, and Stefanie Hoehl. 2021. "Proximity and Touch Are Associated with Neural but Not Physiological Synchrony in Naturalistic Mother-Infant Interactions." *NeuroImage* 244 (December): 118599. https://doi.org/10.1016/j.neuroimage.2021.118599.

Nomikou, Iris, Giuseppe Leonardi, Alicja Radkowska, Joanna Rączaszek-Leonardi, and Katharina J. Rohlfing. 2017. "Taking Up an Active Role: Emerging Participation in Early Mother–Infant Interaction during Peekaboo Routines." *Frontiers in Psychology* 8 (October): 1656. https://doi.org/10.3389/fpsyg.2017.01656.

Oller, D. Kimbrough, Eugene H. Buder, Heather L. Ramsdell, Anne S. Warlaumont, Lesya Chorna, and Roger Bakeman. 2013. "Functional Flexibility of Infant Vocalization and the Emergence of Language." *Proceedings of the National Academy of Sciences* 110 (16): 6318–23. https://doi.org/10.1073/pnas.1300337110.

Oller, D. Kimbrough, Gordon Ramsay, Edina Bene, Helen L. Long, and Ulrike Griebel. 2021. "Protophones, the Precursors to Speech, Dominate the Human Infant Vocal Landscape." *Philosophical Transactions of the Royal Society B* 376 (1836): 20200255.

Oller, D. Kimbrough, Ulrike Griebel, Suneeti Nathani Iyer, Yuna Jhang, Anne S. Warlaumont, Rick Dale, and Josep Call. 2019. "Language Origins Viewed in Spontaneous and Interactive Vocal Rates of Human and Bonobo Infants." *Frontiers in Psychology* 10: 729. https://www.frontiersin.org/journals/psychology/articles/10.3389/fpsyg.2019.00729.

Papoušek, Mechthild. 1995. "Origins of Reciprocity and Mutuality in Prelinguistic Parent-Infant 'Dialogues.'" In *Mutualities in Dialogue*, edited by Ivana Markova, Carl F. Graumann, and Klaus Foppa, 58–81. Cambridge: Cambridge University Press.

Parrino, Liborio, and Anna Elisabetta Vaudano. 2018. "The Resilient Brain and the Guardians of Sleep: New Perspectives on Old Assumptions." *Sleep Medicine Reviews* 39: 98–107.

Perea-Garcia, Juan Olvido, Mariska E. Kret, Antónia Monteiro, and Catherine Hobaiter. 2019. "Scleral Pigmentation Leads to Conspicuous, Not Cryptic, Eye Morphology in Chimpanzees." *Proceedings of the National Academy of Sciences* 116: 19248–50. https://doi.org/10.1073/pnas.1911410116.

Plantinga, Alvin. 1989. *God, Freedom, and Evil*. Grand Rapids, MI: Wm. B. Eerdmans Publishing.

Plantinga, Alvin. 2015. *Knowledge and Christian Belief*. Grand Rapids, MI: Wm. B. Eerdmans.

Poincaré, Henri. 1910. "Mathematical Creation." Translated by George Bruce Halsted. *The Monist* 20 (3): 321–35. https://doi.org/10.1093/monist/20.3.321.

Powell, Lindsey J., Kathryn Hobbs, Alexandros Bardis, Susan Carey, and Rebecca Saxe. 2018. "Replications of Implicit Theory of Mind Tasks with Varying Representational Demands." *Understanding Theory of Mind in Infancy and Toddlerhood* 46 (April): 40–50. https://doi.org/10.1016/j.cogdev.2017.10.004.

Preyer, William T. 1890. *The Mind of the Child: The Development of the Intellect.* New York: Appleton.

Proust, Marcel. 1919. À la *Recherche du Temps Perdu, Tome IV: A l'Ombre des Jeunes Filles en Fleurs, ii.* Paris: Gallimard.

Proust, Marcel. 1923. À la *Recherche du Temps Perdu, Tome VI: La Prisonnière.* Paris: Gallimard.

Raworth, Kate. 2017. *Doughnut Economics: Seven Ways to Think Like a 21st-Century Economist.* London: Random House.

Reddy, Vasudevi. 2008. *How Infants Know Minds.* Cambridge, MA: Harvard University Press.

Reddy, Vasudevi. 2009. "Before the 'Third Element': Understanding Attention to Self." In *Joint Attention: Communication and Other Minds*, edited by Naomi Eilan, Christoph Hoerl, Teresa McCormack, and Johannes Roessler, 85–109. Oxford: Oxford University Press.

Rifkin, Jeremy. 2014. *The Zero Marginal Cost Society: The Internet of Things, the Collaborative Commons, and the Eclipse of Capitalism.* New York: St. Martin's Press.

Riley, Denise. 2004. "'A Voice without a Mouth': Inner Speech." *Qui Parle* 14 (2): 57–104. https://www.jstor.org/stable/20686176.

Rilke, Rainer Maria. 1965/1898. "Über Kunst." In *Sämtliche Werke*. Vol. 5, edited by Ernst Zinn, 426–34. Frankfurt: Insel-Verlag.

Robinson, Ken. 2011. *Out of Our Minds: Learning to Be Creative.* Chichester: John Wiley & Sons.

Rochat, Philippe. 2001. *The Infant's World.* Cambridge, MA: Harvard University Press.

Rochat, Philippe. 2009. *Others in Mind: Social Origins of Self-Consciousness.* New York: Cambridge University Press.

Rogers, Carl Ransom, and Barry Stevens. 1967. *Person to Person: The Problem of Being Human: A New Trend in Psychology.* Moab: Real People Press.

Rovee-Collier, Carolyn. 1997. "Dissociations in Infant Memory: Rethinking the Development of Implicit and Explicit Memory." *Psychological Review* 104 (3): 467–98. https://doi.org/10.1037/0033-295X.104.3.467.

Rowan, John. 2013. *Subpersonalities: The People Inside Us.* New York: Routledge.

Sapolsky, Robert M. 2023. *Determined: Life without Free Will.* New York: Penguin Random House. Kindle Edition.

Sartre, Jean-Paul. 1966/1943. *Being and Nothingness.* Translated by Hazel E. Barnes. New York: Washington Square Press.

Saxe, Rebecca. 2006. "The Forbidden Experiment: What Can We Learn from the Wild Child?" *Boston Review*, August 2006. bostonreview.net/saxe-the-forbidden-experiment.

Schafer, Roy. 1968. *Aspects of Internalization.* New York: International Universities Press, Inc.

Schurger, Aaron, Pengbo "Ben" Hu, Joanna Pak, and Adina L. Roskies. 2021. "What Is the Readiness Potential?" *Trends in Cognitive Sciences* 25 (7): 558–70. https://doi.org/10.1016/j.tics.2021.04.001.

Schutz, Alfred. 1962. *Collected Papers I. The Problem of Social Reality*. The Hague: Martinus Nijhoff.

Scott, Rose M., and Renée Baillargeon. 2017. "Early False-Belief Understanding." *Trends in Cognitive Sciences* 21 (4): 237–49.

Searle, John R. 2007. *Freedom and Neurobiology: Reflections on Free Will, Language, and Political Power*. New York: Columbia University Press.

Seifert, Colleen M., David E. Meyer, Natalie Davidson, Andrea L. Patalano, and Ilan Yaniv. 1995. "Demystification of Cognitive Insight: Opportunistic Assimilation and the Prepared-Mind Perspective." In *The Nature of Insight*, edited by Robert J. Sternberg and Janet E. Davidson, 65–124. Cambridge: MIT Press.

Simms, Eva M. 2008. *The Child in the World: Embodiment, Time, and Language in Early Childhood*. Detroit: Wayne State University Press.

Sinha, Pawan, Margaret M. Kjelgaard, Tapan K. Gandhi, Kleovoulos Tsourides, Annie L. Cardinaux, Dimitrios Pantazis, Sidney P. Diamond, and Richard M. Held. 2014. "Autism as a Disorder of Prediction." *Proceedings of the National Academy of Sciences* 111 (42): 15220–25. https://doi.org/10.1073/pnas.1416797111.

Sloman, Aaron, and Ronald Chrisley. 2003. "Virtual Machines and Consciousness." *Journal of Consciousness Studies* 10 (4–5): 133–72.

Smith, David Livingstone. 2011. *Less than Human: Why We Demean, Enslave, and Exterminate Others*. New York: St. Martin's Press.

Southgate, Victoria. 2020. "Are Infants Altercentric? The Other and the Self in Early Social Cognition." *Psychological Review* 127 (4): 505–23. https://doi.org/10.1037/rev0000182.

Stawarska, Beata. 2009. "Dialogue at the Limit of Phenomenology." *Chiasmi International* 11 (July): 145–56. https://doi.org/10.5840/chiasmi20091128.

Stein, Edith. 1989. *On the Problem of Empathy*. Translated by Waltraut Stein. 3rd ed. Washington, DC: ICS.

Stern, Daniel N. 1985. *The Interpersonal World of the Infant*. New York: Basic Books.

Stern, Daniel N. 1989. "Crib Monologues from a Psychoanalytic Perspective." In *Narratives from the Crib*, edited by Katherine Nelson, 309–19. Cambridge, MA: Harvard University Press.

Strawson, P. F. 1959. *Individuals: An Essay in Descriptive Metaphysics*. London: Methuen.

Sylvester, David. 2012. *About Modern Art: Critical Essays 1948–2000*. Revised ed. London: Random House.

Teague, Samantha J., Kylie M. Gray, Bruce J. Tonge, and Louise K. Newman. 2017. "Attachment in Children with Autism Spectrum Disorder: A Systematic

Review." *Research in Autism Spectrum Disorders* 35 (March): 35–50. https://doi.org/10.1016/j.rasd.2016.12.002.

Terrace, Herbert S., Ann E. Bigelow, and Beatrice Beebe. 2022. "Intersubjectivity and the Emergence of Words." *Frontiers in Psychology* 13: 693139.

Thompson, Evan. 2015. *Waking, Dreaming, Being*. New York: Columbia University Press.

Tillotson, Geoffrey, and Kathleen Tillotson. 2013. *Mid-Victorian Studies*. London: Bloomsbury.

Tomasello, Michael. 1999. "Social Cognition before the Revolution." In *Early Social Cognition: Understanding Others in the First Months of Life*, edited by Philippe Rochat, 301–14. New York: Psychology Press.

Tomasello, Michael. 2003. *Constructing a Language: A Usage-Based Approach to Child Language Acquisition*. Cambridge, MA: Harvard University Press.

Tomasello, Michael. 2014. *A Natural History of Human Thinking*. Cambridge, MA: Harvard University Press.

Tomasello, Michael. 2019. *Becoming Human: A Theory of Ontogeny*. Cambridge, MA: Harvard University Press.

Tooley, Michael. 2021. "The Problem of Evil." In *The Stanford Encyclopedia of Philosophy*, Winter 2021 Ed., edited by Edward N. Zalta. Stanford University, Stanford, CA: Metaphysics Research Lab. https://plato.stanford.edu/archives/win2021/entries/evil/.

Trehub, Sandra E., Anna M. Unyk, and Laurel J. Trainor. 1993. "Maternal Singing in Cross-Cultural Perspective." *Infant Behavior and Development* 16 (3): 285–95. https://doi.org/10.1016/0163-6383(93)80036-8.

Trevarthen, Colwyn. 1977. "Descriptive Analyses of Infant Communicative Behaviour." In *Studies in Mother-Infant Interaction*, edited by H. Rudolph Schaffer, 227–70. London: Academic Press.

Trevarthen, Colwyn. 1993. "The Self Born in Intersubjectivity: The Psychology of an Infant Communicating." In *The Perceived Self: Ecological and Interpersonal Sources of Self-Knowledge*, edited by Ulrich Neisser, 121–73. New York: Cambridge University Press.

Tronick, Edward Z. 1989. "Emotions and Emotional Communication in Infants." *American Psychologist* 44 (2): 112–19. https://doi.org/10.1037/0003-066X.44.2.112.

Tronick, Edward Z. 2009. *The Neurobehavioral and Social-Emotional Development of Infants and Children*. New York: WW Norton & Company.

Twain, Mark. 1885. *The Adventures of Huckleberry Finn*. London: Chatto & Windus/Webster.

Waldenfels, Bernhard. 1971. *Das Zwischenreich des Dialogs: Sozial-Philosophische Untersuchungen in Anschluss am Edmund Husserl*. The Hague: Martinus Nijhoff.

Weber, Max. 1958/1904–1905. *The Protestant Ethic and the Spirit of Capitalism*. New York: Scribner.

Wilson, Arnold, and Lissa Weinstein. 1990. "Language, Thought, and Interiorization: A Vygotskian and Psychoanalytic Perspective." *Contemporary Psychoanalysis* 26 (1): 24–40. https://doi.org/10.1080/00107530.1990.10746637.

Winnicott, D. W. 1965. *The Maturational Processes and the Facilitating Environment: Studies in the Theory of Emotional Development.* London: The Hogarth Press and the Institute of Psycho-Analysis.

Wittgenstein, Ludwig. 1980. *Remarks on the Philosophy of Psychology II.* Translated by C. Grant Luckhardt and Maximilian A. E. Aue. Vol. II. Oxford: Blackwell.

Woolf, Virginia. 1929. *A Room of One's Own.* London: The Hogarth Press.

Wörmann, Viktoriya, Manfred Holodynski, Joscha Kärtner, and Heidi Keller. 2012. "A Cross-Cultural Comparison of the Development of the Social Smile." *Infant Behavior and Development* 35 (3): 335–47. https://doi.org/10.1016/j.infbeh.2012.03.002.

Zahavi, Dan. 1999. *Self-Awareness and Alterity.* Evanston, IL: Northwestern University Press.

Zahavi, Dan. 2014. *Self and Other: Exploring Subjectivity, Empathy, and Shame.* New York: Oxford University Press.

Zeiträg, Claudia, Thomas Rejsenhus Jensen, and Mathias Osvath. 2022. "Gaze Following: A Socio-Cognitive Skill Rooted in Deep Time." *Frontiers in Psychology* 13: 950935. https://doi.org/10.3389/fpsyg.2022.950935.

Zoia, Stefania, Laura Blason, Giuseppina D'Ottavio, Maria Bulgheroni, Eva Pezzetta, Aldo Scabar, and Umberto Castiello. 2007. "Evidence of Early Development of Action Planning in the Human Foetus: A Kinematic Study." *Experimental Brain Research* 176 (2): 217–26. https://doi.org/10.1007/s00221-006-0607-3.

Index

For Product Safety Concerns and Information please contact our EU
representative GPSR@taylorandfrancis.com
Taylor & Francis Verlag GmbH, Kaufingerstraße 24, 80331 München, Germany